40 Days of Repentance:
A Companion Guide to The LIST

Edited by
Laura Densmore

Co-authored by
Laura Densmore
Ray Montgomery
Bob O'Dell

With Contributions from:
Nathalie Blackham
Linda Chandler
Thomas and Amy Cogdell
Jeff Daly
Christine Darg
Cathy Helms
Donna Jollay
Albert J. McCarn
Amy Mucklestone
Sharon Sanders
Sister Joela
Sister Damiana
Steve Wearp

Published by
ROOT SOURCE PRESS

ROOT
SOURCE

PRESS

First Edition

40 Days of Repentance: A Companion Guide to The LIST

For permission requests, write to the publisher, with the subject
"Attention: Permissions Coordinator," and send to the below address.
Root Source Press
Love of the Land Street #1
Maale Hever, DN Har Hebron 90420 ISRAEL
rspress@root-source.com
www.root-source.com

ROOT
SOURCE

PRESS

Special discounts are available for churches, book clubs, corporations, associations, resellers, trade bookstores, and wholesalers. For details contact the publisher at the above address.

The authors are available to speak at your church, fundraiser or special event.

Printed in the United States of America
Cover design, illustrations and layout by Arnulfo and Bituin Aquino
arn.aquino@gmail.com

ISBN: 978-965-7738-12-2

This publication is designed to provide accurate and authoritative information in regard to the subject matter covered. It is sold with the understanding that the authors or the publisher are not engaged in rendering any type of professional services. If assistance is required, the services of a competent professional should be sought. Effort has been made to verify accurate Internet addresses. The authors and the publisher assume no responsibility for Internet address errors.

1. Judaism 2. Christianity 2. Bible Study 3. Bible Commentary 4. Repentance 5. 9th of Av
6. Church Forefathers 7. Jewish History 8. Tisha b'Av

I. Densmore, Laura, O'Dell, Bob and Montgomery, Raymond
II. 40 Days of Repentance: A Companion Guide to The LIST

TABLE OF CONTENTS

Introduction: 40 Days

by Gidon Ariel

The number 40 has great significance in Judaism.

Consider:

- In the story of Noah, it famously rained for 40 days and 40 nights.
- Moses was on Mount Sinai for 40 days and 40 nights. His stay there concluded with his coming down with tablets of stone, engraved with the Ten Commandments.
- In Deuteronomy 25:3, the Bible commands that when a rabbinical court finds someone guilty of a crime, the punishment is sometimes lashes, prescribed in the Torah as "forty less one."
- The spies toured the Land of Canaan for 40 days.
- Moses led the Jewish people for 40 years in the wilderness.
- Three times in the book of Judges, the phrase "and the land was quiet for 40 years" appears.
- According to the sages (Mishna, Chapters of the Fathers 5:26), at age 40 a person reaches the level of binah - deep insight.
- There are 40 days between the first day of Elul, when we begin to blow the Shofar to prepare for Rosh Hashana, until Yom Kippur, the end of the annual teshuva (repentance) period. These 40 days are the most auspicious time for personal growth and renewal.[1]

What is the significance of this number? What do these stories and events have in common?

It is quite obvious that in each episode, there was a drastic change between the status quo before the 40 and after it. But note: some were a significant upgrade, and some were a tragic downfall.

This perhaps can be associated with the Hebrew letter that has a numerical value of 40: Mem. The name of that letter means water (Mayim), and similarly water can go either of two ways after a long period: it can either boil or freeze.

There is yet another natural period that is associated with 40: there are 40 weeks of pregnancy, after which a child is born. But it is still unclear at birth whether that child will be righteous, or, God forbid, otherwise.

I think that God is hinting to us, through Scripture, history and nature, that any situation can be focused on and changed for the better. It is, in fact, a well documented Internet fact that it takes 40 days to break a habit. Of course, as Abraham Lincoln said, "don't believe everything you read", but the concept of focusing on something for a significant amount of time is self-evident.

As he wrote in this book, my friend and partner at Root Source Bob O'Dell came across the phenomenon of Christian antisemitism and persecution of Jews years ago, and this changed his life. Through research, he compiled a first draft of what would become The LIST: Christian Persecution of Jews Throughout History, and the volume you hold is a companion to it. But Bob realized that dry research is not enough. He needed to consider The LIST, to meditate on it, to pray about it.

And pray he did. I will leave exactly what format Bob's prayer took and what impact it had upon him for his own chapters, but I am here to set the stage for you, dear reader, to benefit from Bob's work (and later on, Ray's and Laura's too).

For many Christians, it is a shock to learn that the Church or individual Christians committed acts of terror against Jews. How could anyone with any relationship whatsoever with the Prince of Peace resort to prejudice, hatred, violence, and even murder? Some even deal with this cognitive dissonance by denying that the perpetrators were even Christian.

But this excuse cannot be accepted. As The LIST so clearly and emphatically demonstrates, this antisemitism passed over no category of Christians. Taking ownership of a spiritual or cultural relationship to these people is the first step in taking their acts seriously, repenting for them, and ultimately helping the entire body of Christ to repent and change course from this horrible sin, which so clearly is a required goal for achieving God's Kingdom on Earth.

The three main authors of this book, Bob, Ray and Laura, spared no emotional effort in producing the lion's share of prayers and meditations to go along with repenting for Christian antisemitism. They further reached out to Christian leaders worldwide who immediately responded favorably to their invitation to join in the composition of these articles.

We encourage you, dear reader, to dare to commit to join these leaders and pray these chapters, one a day for 40 days, leading up to the tragic "holiday" of Tisha B'Av, the ninth day of the Hebrew month of Av, the saddest day on the Jewish calendar. Alternatively, you can time your reading to conclude on Yom Kippur, the Biblical Day of Atonement. In 2019, these dates are July 2 - August 11, or August 30 - October 9. For subsequent years, see https://9-av.com/40-day-calendar. Please join the conversation there as well, and add your comments.

Now that you've read this far into the Introduction, you are probably wondering who I am. Perhaps you could say I am an example of what a movement of Christians internalizing the messages of this book and The LIST can do to a Jew.

I was born in New York, in a standard, traditional Jewish family, which among other things means that we stayed together with other Jews and always kept our distance from anyone else, which usually meant Christians. But soon after my twentieth birthday, I discovered pro-Jewish Christian organizations, like the International Christian Embassy Jerusalem, Bridges for Peace, Christian Friends of Israel, and others. And because of my natural tendency to be friendly, I reached out to these Christians, and was met with a warm, sincere, no-strings-attached willingness and interest to just be friends! Imagine that, Jews and Christians have such great differences, but much in common as well! Ultimately that is what it all boils down to, as the prophet Malachi states:

Aren't all children of the same Father? Weren't we all created by the same God? Why should we betray each other? MALACHI 2:10 (NLT)

This realization, and especially the warm and sincere friendships that I discovered and came to treasure, helped me to establish with my (then new) friend Bob O'Dell our organization Root Source. At Root Source, Jews and Christians focus on what they have in common: building friendships, learning the roots of their faith, and pursuing goals they share in common. Please join us at www.Root-Source.com.

Gidon Ariel

Publisher, Root Source Press
February 2019
Hebron, Israel

ENDNOTES:

1. http://www.aish.com/atr/The_Number_40.html

From the Timeline to The LIST

by Ray Montgomery

"Then you will know the truth, and the truth will set you free."
JOHN 8:32 (NIV)

In 2008 I began compiling a Christian Timeline to get a sense of the "Big Picture" of our Church history. In 2010 I began researching Jewish history as well, to flesh out the empty gaps in my Timeline. Little did I know where this intellectual pursuit would lead.

Ray Montgomery standing next to his Christian Timeline.

Jewish History

Jews have been faithfully recording scripture for millennia, so it made sense that they would faithfully record their history as well. The more I researched the more I noticed an ugly truth: most of these atrocities had been carried out by Christian nations, or Christians acting "in the name of Christ".

While I was aware of the broad brushstrokes of our bloody history covering the Inquisition, the Crusades, Jewish expulsions, and the Holocaust, why wasn't I aware of these other atrocities?

Combing through these websites year-by-year, century-by-century, the feelings of guilt and disgust had a compounding effect. When I finished, I was undone. For days I could say nothing. I felt sick to my stomach. I descended into what I at first thought was deep depression, but later realised was deep grief. Even though I hadn't committed any of these acts myself, why was I feeling so guilty? Why had it taken a painful 3-month examination of Jewish history to discover this?

All I could think of was the latter part of Exodus 34:7:

> *"...Yet he does not leave the guilty unpunished; he punishes the children and their children for the sin of the parents to the third and fourth generation."* (NIV)

The Journey of Repentance

I finally realised that the sins my Church forefathers had committed against the Jews, and which was now weighing heavily on my shoulders, was their collective guilt becoming personal. All I could do was to cry out to the LORD in repentance, seeking His forgiveness. It took weeks to be released from two millennia's worth of guilt. And it broke me.

But this journey also gave me compassion for the Jews, so whenever I met a Jewish person, I explained what I had learned, apologised to them for the sins of my Church forefathers, and asked them for their forgiveness personally. And each time I have always been surprised at how loving and forgiving they were to me. If anybody should be angry and want to seek revenge (and have the right to exact some kind of revenge!), it is the Jews. And yet every time they have shown such grace, forgiveness and compassion towards me that I feel truly humbled.

This led to actively speaking out for the Jews, stopping antisemitism in its tracks, using the knowledge I've gained to rebut misinformed people's attitudes and beliefs.

And finally it led to reaching out to Bob O'Dell in March 2018, in the hopes that he would "do something". Little did I know where that innocent email would lead!

Reaching out to Bob O'Dell

In 2015 Bob published his video series on the Blood Moons. In Part Four: Valleys and Shadows[1], he revealed how he began researching the Christian persecution of Jews. I noticed the parallel with my own journey, but it wasn't until reviewing them again in March that I felt compelled to contact him. I had always wanted this knowledge to be more widely disseminated, so I suggested that with Root Source's global reach and Bob's journalistic skills, perhaps he might like to "do something" about it:

> "So here's my suggestion: in preparation for the upcoming 9th of Av anniversary (July 21-22 2018), why don't you do a series of teachings on this date and its significance, and migrate this onto a summary of Christian persecution of our Jewish brethren in general, and the need for global corporate repentance?"

Bob's reply:

> "A man (you) asks another man (me) to do something that God puts on his (your) heart. Then the first man is assigned a bunch of tasks by the second man to see if he is willing to get involved and do some work regarding that idea. Funny how that works, isn't it? And yet it seems quite fitting to me!"

Very fitting indeed. But little did we know where the fruits of our combined research would lead!

It led to our collaboration together on The LIST! Together with a signed Declaration of Repentance by 2,000 people, they were presented to the Speaker of the Israeli Knesset, Yuli Edelstein, by a delegation of Christians, in time for the 9th of Av 2018. And from those auspicious beginnings came this book of devotions based on The LIST, with plans to gather in Jerusalem in August 2019 on the 9th of Av for a solemn assembly!

The last step in the journey is to make restitution, to bless Israel. It has been my privilege to be part of this project of Repentance, to collaborate with Bob and present our findings in The LIST, thereby "getting the word out". It has also been my privilege to write some of these devotions, and it is my prayer that the LORD will use them to bring about global corporate Christian repentance for the sins of our Church forefathers. And may the proceeds of both these books be a small gesture of restitution from us to the Jewish people.

Will you pray this repentance prayer with me?

Heavenly Father,

Thank You for sending Your Son to this world, that through Him we might be saved and be able to follow You. Thank You for guiding our lives in such a way as to lead us on a path that is unique to each of us.

Father, when our path takes an unexpected turn, You are still faithful to lead us in paths of righteousness for Your name's sake. Together we are on a path that is itself that "unexpected turn", for who among us can say that we had full knowledge of the sins that have been committed in the name of Christ?

Please lead us and guide us in the path we are on -- the path of repentance. Show us in the days ahead how we can be part of an effort to repent for the sins of our Church forefathers, and to do so with urgency for the sake of the Church worldwide. Lead, guide and comfort all of those who are joining together on this journey of repentance, and effect within us the full measure of response, and lead us into Your sweet embrace as well.

Help us to embrace the fellowship of the suffering You've had to witness.

Bless the Jewish people, and allow us to be those who would stand with them in love, and to demonstrate love to them in tangible ways.

And as we embrace our history, and embrace this journey, may we experience the reality of knowing the truth, which will set us free indeed.

In Jesus' precious name,

Amen.

ENDNOTES:

1. https://root-source.com/blog/valleys-and-shadows-the-blood-moons-course-part-four/

40 days to 9-av 2019
Day 1: July 3, 2019

40 days to Yom Kippur 2019
Day 1: August 31, 2019

Fill in the blank
Day 1: _____

The Evil Report of the Ten Spies at Kadesh Barnea

by Laura Densmore

Many evil things have happened to the Jewish people over the centuries, and not just on any random day, but on the 9th of Av. How did this get started? And, more importantly, how might this day of sorrow and grief one day become a day of joy and gladness as it is written in Zechariah?

> *"Thus saith the LORD of hosts; The fast of the fourth month, and the fast of the fifth, and the fast of the seventh, and the fast of the tenth, shall be to the house of Judah joy and gladness, and cheerful feasts; therefore love the truth and peace."* ZECHARIAH 8:19 (KJV)

The very first event on The LIST is the incident that happened at Kadesh Barnea. The rabbis teach that the evil report given by the ten spies did not happen on any random day: it happened on the 9th of Av:

> *"And Caleb stilled the people before Moses, and said, Let us go up at once, and possess it; for we are well able to overcome it. But the men that went up with him said, We be not able to go up against the people; for they are stronger than we. And they brought up an evil report of the land which they had searched unto the children of Israel, saying, The land, through which we have gone to search it, is a land that eats up the inhabitants thereof; and all the people that we saw in it are men of a great stature. And there we saw the giants, the sons of Anak, which come of the giants: and we were in our own sight as grasshoppers, and so we were in their sight."* NUMBERS 13:30-33 (KJV)

The sin of the ten spies was their "evil report"; their negative words they spoke to the people. What was the sin of the people? The people chose to believe the words of this evil report, instead of believing and trusting God's word and His promise to them. They walked right into the sin of UNBELIEF in the Word of God.

There was a severe consequence for their unbelief: that generation would not cross over into the Promised Land but instead would wander and then die in the wilderness:

> *"And your children shall wander in the wilderness forty years, and bear your whoredoms, until your carcases be wasted in the wilderness. After the number of the days in which ye searched the land, even forty days, each day for a year, shall ye bear your iniquities, even forty years, and **ye shall know my breach of promise.**"* NUMBERS 14:33-34 (KJV, emphasis mine)

Their own sin had caused a "breach" in God's promise to them. A measure for measure judgment was issued from the courtroom of heaven: for the 40 days they spent exploring the land, they would now spend 40 *years* wandering in the wilderness.

The word for "evil report" is *"dibbah,"* which means: defamation, whispering, or evil report. Who were the ten spies defaming in this evil report? They were defaming the nature and character of God Himself! Their lack of trust in His promise was treachery against the God of Israel!

This evil report spoken out brought fear, doubt and unbelief into the hearts and minds and of the people. The evil report spread throughout the camp like wildfire. They heard the words of this evil report, and then came into agreement with it, and thus came into the sin of unbelief. They did not trust the LORD at His Word, and at His promise. What had He promised them?

> *"As for Me, behold, My covenant is with you, and you shall be a father of many nations. No longer shall your name be called Abram, but your name shall be Abraham; for I have made you a father of many nations. I will make you exceedingly fruitful; and I will make nations of you, and kings shall come from you. And I will establish My covenant between Me and you and your descendants after you in their generations, for an everlasting covenant, to be God to you and your descendants after you. Also I give to you and your descendants after you the land in which you are a stranger, all the land of Canaan, as an everlasting possession; and I will be their God."*
> GENESIS 17:4-8 (KJV)

Pictured above: Abraham's seed to be more numerous than the stars.

The people wept all that night, and by the next day, they were ready to pack up their bags and go back to Egypt rather than press forward with the LORD into the Promised Land!

The horrible history against the Jewish people for the last 2,000 years started with the sin of the Israelites all the way back in Kadesh Barnea. It might be easy today to look back at the lack of faith by the Israelites in Kadesh Barnea and to point our fingers at them in judgment.

However, as we read through early Church history, a pattern emerges. In reading through The LIST you will see that even "the best" Church fathers did not believe the Word of God that was given to Moses at Mt. Sinai. They did not accept the covenant promises as still applying!

It is our assertion in this book of devotions that one of the root sins that led to many of the atrocities against the Jews in the name of Christ, was the sin of unbelief — unbelief in God's Word. It is this unbelief in God's Word, especially unbelief in the Hebrew scriptures (or Old Testament) that gave rise to Replacement Theology; and it is Replacement Theology that has been a powerful driving force underlying the persecution against Jewish people over the centuries.

Yet, may I offer a ray of hope as we begin this 40-day journey of repentance together?

Could it be that as we embark on this 40-day repentance journey, that somehow the Father can redeem the 40 years of wandering in the wilderness that the Israelites went through at Kadesh Barnea?

Could it be that as we purpose and choose to walk in faith in the God of Israel and in the fullness of His Word that the sin of unbelief in the Church can somehow be redeemed?

The original "breach of promise" was caused by the Israelites' sin of unbelief. Perhaps this breach can be repaired and the promise renewed by our walking out this 40-day repentance journey in faithfulness and in obedience!

Let us begin that journey and see what the God of Israel will do!

Will you pray this repentance prayer with me?

Heavenly Father,

We stand in the gap and we repent on behalf of the Israelites at Kadesh Barnea. We repent for the sin of unbelief in which they walked. They did not trust You! They did not believe Your Word and Your Covenant promise that You made to them.

Further down the river of time, we confess that our Church forefathers did not believe the Word of God as it was given to Moses at Mt. Sinai. We repent for the sin of unbelief in the Word of God in the lives of our Church forefathers. We also repent for the sin of unbelief in our own lives and for the sin of unbelief in the Church today!

Would You please help us, Father, to have unshakable, unwavering rock solid faith in You and in Your Word? May we believe and trust in Your WORD more than what our eyes see, and more than what our circumstances say to us.

Abba, as we embark upon this journey of repentance for the next 40 days, we are asking You that for each day that we repent, would You roll back one of the 40 years of judgment so that at the end of the 40 days, the 40 years of judgment would become 40 days of FAITHFULNESS and OBEDIENCE that You find in Your people?

Through these next 40 days, would You redeem those 40 years and bring forth blessing and breakthrough?

Abba, we are resolved to be people who will keep our eyes on You, on the God of Israel. You are good, and You are full of mercy, compassion, and loving kindness. You do not lie. Your Word is sure, it is true, and it stands forever. Our eyes are upon You. We love You and we are resolved to TRUST in You, and in Your Word: all of it, from Genesis to Revelation!

In Yeshua's name,

Amen and amen!

Undone

by Bob O'Dell

I still remember the feeling I felt in April of 2013 — the feeling of a racehorse being let out of a starting gate and running with purpose and yet abandon. Here I was in my early 50s, having just left my electronics career behind, and for the first time ever, setting aside the next nine months to find out what was that next big task that God had in store for me. I knew that living for one's self isn't a winning long term plan, and I was looking forward to decompressing from a hectic work and travel schedule to be free to explore "whatever".

One of my interests was End Times prophecy, and in those days, some of the most interesting theories being talked about were ideas having to do with Israel: the Blood Moons, the Seven Year Shemitah cycle, and so forth. I had spent the last twenty-five years working with Israelis in the high-tech arena and had visited Israel often. But now I would have time to pursue Israel from a more Christian angle. I quickly learned that to study these topics, I was going to need to fill a big hole in my education: history. I was woefully understudied in the topic of world history in general, and Israel and Christian history in particular, at least during the post-biblical period of the last 2,000 years.

In the process of studying that history, I learned about the horrible and amazing pattern of Jewish tragedies that had occurred on the 9th day of the fifth month on the Jewish Calendar, the 9th of Av. Here are a few of them as mentioned in The LIST:

- The destruction of the First Temple by Nebuchadnezzar in 586 BCE

- The destruction of the Second Temple by Rome in 70 CE

- The crushing of the Jewish Revolt of 135 CE

- The day the First Crusade began in 1096 CE

- The day that England expelled the Jews in 1290 CE

- The day that Spain expelled the Jews in 1492 CE

- The day that Himmler received approval for The Final Solution plan in 1941 CE

Pictured above: Destruction of the Second Temple in 70 AD.

After reading the basics on the last 2,000 years of history, I went back and read specifically about Jewish and Christian history from various viewpoints — Catholic, Protestant, Messianic, secular and Orthodox: about fifty history books in all. I was really getting into this now! I began to see that the relationship between Christians and Jews was a lot more, shall we say, *complex* than I had realized.

I began to catalog specific events of persecution towards Christians and Jews. Every time I came across a new location and date of persecution, I would drop it into a spreadsheet and add a brief description. I quickly discovered that the events perpetrated against Jews were going to overwhelm the other categories. I was expecting the various books I was reading to be repeating the same basic persecution events over and over, but instead, every time I read another book, I discovered new persecution events against Jews.

And then came the 9th of Av in the summer of 2013. Now that I understood its history, and why the Jewish people would choose this day to fast and pray, I came upon an idea: what if I were to halt my own study of history for one day, and examine the events perpetrated against the Jews?

I opened my Excel spreadsheet, and saw to my disbelief that this file now had about 500 incidents spread over its many pages! Oh my! Even if I only spent "one minute" on each of them, this was going to take a full eight hours!

I decided to do exactly that: my task on the 9th of Av of 2013 would be to fast like the Jews do, and then to examine each row for one minute, consider it, and move to the next. For example:

- A particular pogrom: e.g. 414 CE

- A particular killing: e.g. 1096

- A particular riot against Jewish homes: e.g 1190

- Forcing Jews to wear special clothing: e.g. 1259

- An expulsion of Jews from a town or region: e.g. from France in 1182

- Special laws going into effect to restrict Jewish life: e.g. 306

- Restriction of employment: e.g. 1310

- An antisemitic writing from a Church Father: e.g. 386

- A humiliation: e.g. 1195

- A burning of Jewish books: e.g. 681

- A mob attack: e.g. 1147

- A blaming of Jews for a natural disaster: e.g. 1020

- A blaming of Jews for a plague: e.g. 1348

- A blaming of Jews for random killings: e.g. 1287

- A burning of a synagogue: e.g. 1221

- The pouring of human blood upon their matzah: e.g. 1270

For one minute each I would think about what was written on a particular row. I would try to imagine what it would be like to have been present and to have watched those things happen. Then I would move on to the next.

I sat down in my study chair at eight o'clock that Tuesday morning on July 16th, 2013 and began. It was not too difficult at first. But as the day rolled on, the events just kept coming and coming. Not only was I thinking about what the Jewish people had endured, but I also considered the fact that this particular row in my spreadsheet (all but a few of them) had never been known to me. How was it that I had never heard it mentioned in my entire Christian life, nor from any of the Israeli Jews that I had worked with almost daily for over twenty-five years?

"Why had I never known this?" I asked over and over that day.

As I read hundreds of these events in order, from about the second century onward, the vile acts just continued to get worse and worse. This was clearly the most unusual fast in which I had ever partaken. At some point in the 1200s in the early afternoon, I could no longer even sit and read. I became physically ill and had to stop. I never even reached the horrible events in the later centuries! I was overwhelmed by the atrocities committed against the Jews by my European Christian forefathers.

Then I suddenly realized something else — something that I was not seeing: There was no record of Jews ever repaying evil for evil in what they suffered from us.

I was undone.

I was undone by historical truth, and I was not even halfway through my nine-month project!

In the weeks that followed I began to grapple with how I might respond to that which I had learned. My response need not be the same as yours. We are all unique individuals before God. But I am pleased to say that God helped me find my way forward. It turns out that for me, the next big task that God had in store for me would be to go back to Israel — this time not to meet with Israeli electronics engineers, but to meet with Orthodox Jews to see if there was any way that my business experience could be of help to them. By January 2014, and after a long list of consecutive "coincidences", I met Orthodox Jew Gidon Ariel on the walls of Jerusalem and heard him share an idea he had to teach the Bible to Christians from an authentically Jewish perspective. Gidon's vision would become Root Source, eventually the publisher of The LIST and the book you are now holding.

But this is not Gidon's first book to publish. That honor belongs to another book: *Israel FIRST!*, co-written by Gidon and myself, in which I shared a longer version of the story you just read.

Then in 2018 a man named Ray Montgomery, having read my story, contacted me and told me that he went through a very similar experience as mine, but three years earlier. Our discussions led to the combining of our respective research and the publishing of a document that we now call The LIST; just in time for the 9th of Av in 2018.

Your life story is precious before God. It is as precious as mine. I believe that if you live your life fully before God, and I live mine fully then together God will weave our stories together in a way that will help mend the great rift that has split the Jewish world from the Christian world. You don't *have* to visit Israel to do it, although God may certainly lead you to visit in due time. You just have to fulfill *your* purpose. The divide between Christians and Jews is so wide that it is going to take people like you and me to mend it. And I cannot think of a better next step for you and for me over the next 40 days, than immersing yourself in this devotional, which contains some of the most thought-provoking ideas and personal stories that you may ever read.

Will you pray this repentance prayer with me?

Father in Heaven,

As we walk along this 40-day path of repentance, would You do the work within each of us that would be pleasing to You?

Would You bring us into a place of preparation to take the matter of our history seriously, and lead us in ways to pray that we may never have thought of before? Guide our hearts. Guide our steps. Lead us in the everlasting way and into the fullness of your peace.

We pray for the peace of Jerusalem right now, and ask that we might be an agent of peace in Your plan for Jerusalem, Israel and the World.

In Yeshua's name, we pray.

Amen.

The Fellowship of His Suffering

by Ray Montgomery

"That I may know Him and the power of His resurrection and the fellowship of His sufferings, being conformed to His death." PHILIPPIANS 3:10 (NASB)

"But Jesus said to them, 'You don't know what you are asking! Are you able to drink from the bitter cup of suffering I am about to drink? Are you able to be baptized with the baptism of suffering I must be baptized with?'"
MARK 10:38 (NLT)

In 2010, when I began researching Jewish history, I had no idea where it would lead. But after 3 months of intensive research, I was simply overwhelmed, and sank into what I thought was deep depression, but later realised was *deep grief*. This ultimately led to a personal journey of repentance, which in turn led to a heart reconciliation with my Jewish brethren, which in turn led to contacting Bob O'Dell in March 2018 (for he too had done this same journey), which in turn led to a collaboration with him to compile The LIST from both our resources, which in turn led Laura Densmore to contact us after she'd read The LIST and been deeply affected by it, which in turn led to these 40 daily devotions.

But further research to prepare for version 2.0 of The LIST has led to several personal "meltdowns" (for want of a better word), which is the only word that adequately describes the effects of finding out yet more atrocities of our Christian past. And each time I found myself asking, can this possibly get any worse?

Sometimes it was just the volume of vitriol our Church forefathers had written that would get me down, which is what happened the day I wrote the devotion "Sowing and Reaping". At first I didn't know what to do with this. I couldn't keep on repenting. So I contacted a friend to ask for prayer for spiritual protection for the work I was doing. At some point in the conversation he asked me if it was possible that I was not under attack, but that perhaps I was being allowed by Christ himself, to experience the *fellowship of His suffering*.

The more I thought about this, the more I realised that this was exactly what it was: the journey of repentance had now led to sharing in the *fellowship of His suffering!* As this dawned on me I broke down and wept uncontrollably.

A few weeks later, while reading the "Janowska Road" story (which I recount in detail in the devotion, "The Holocaust"), I unexpectedly found my spirit being crushed by the hardness of heart in the perpetrators who would not let go of the notion that their hatred of the Jews was nothing less than the fulfilment of a "great service" to their "God".

Again I descended to a dark place. This time I began writing. This happens each time that I add more, such as after reading *Adversus Judaeos* ("Against the Jews") by St. John Chrysostom, a Doctor of the Church and one of the four Great Greek Fathers. These eight homilies (*see entries on The LIST, 386-87*) denounce Jews and Judaising Christians, casting Jews as a demon-possessed people who could never be forgiven, and it was therefore the responsibility of Christians to hate Jews! And he used scripture to "justify" every point he made.

Each time I sank into this deep state of grief, I continued writing to try and make sense of what was happening. I finally ended up penning these words:

> "It's a dark, black place. And bleak. Your face betrays your emotions. It's like something unpleasant has settled in the pit of your stomach, and just won't budge. Words are not only inadequate; they are unnecessary, futile, and even get in the way. The only thing you can do is endure it, and let it do what it needs to do.

> It feels like a spirit of heaviness has enveloped you, a spirit of sadness has clothed you, and your spirit in turn feels utterly crushed by the weight of this burden. "A wounded spirit, who can bear?" Solomon cried.

> Wallowing around in the history of our Christian sewers leaves the same sort of dirty, filthy "ick" factor the foul, fetid imagery conveys, lasting long after the first contact in reading about the event.

> This "ick" factor is the weight of millennia of grief, witnessed by Him

and a cloud of unseen witnesses, but borne by Him alone. It's this grief that He needs to share, and this is His invitation to join Him. It's a lonely, deeply personal place He is inviting you to, a quiet place to fellowship with Him in His sufferings. And in this place, you become aware that your own spirit itself is weeping in concert with Him. But eventually, even those inner tears seep through while you grieve. And even when your tears dry up, your spirit is still crying.

It feels horrible, like it will never end. You can't repent from it, get forgiven, and move on; you can't rebuke it; you can't escape it. You just have to endure it, and let it runs its course. And as it does, and as your day moves on, it continues to overshadow things, always percolating at the back of your mind, always present in some unseen way, permeating and punctuating your thoughts. But over time, the more it happens, you find yourself becoming a quieter person, softer, gentler; more conformed to His image.

Knowing that He needs you to share it with Him makes it no less painful, but at least bearable. And in that place of deeply personal, intimate fellowship, an inexorable change unfolds deep in your spirit, an indelible change that undeniably changes you. Forever."

I find that these moments come along quite unexpectedly. I can be reading something in The LIST, and suddenly it happens. Or I can be driving, and find myself weeping uncontrollably over something I had read earlier. All I can do is to encourage you to do what I have done: take it to Him, and let it go where it goes.

So if an entry in The LIST "grabs" you, for whatever reason, or after you've read one of these daily devotions, go back to the entry in The LIST, click on the links, read what the articles say, and research some more. We are so blessed to live in an age where we have access to knowledge at our fingertips. But this is a double edged-sword, for with knowledge comes responsibility. So lose yourself in the story; then withdraw to that quiet place, and lose yourself in Him. Even though the event may have been something that happened a long, long time ago, own the sin, and repent as if it were yours and yours alone. And don't be afraid to go where it goes. Tears will inevitably flow. Grieve with Him, and learn to share in the fellowship of His suffering.

Jesus said, at the darkest moment of His life just before His crucifixion:

"Father, if you are willing, remove this cup from me. Nevertheless, not my will, but yours, be done." LUKE 22:42 (WEB)

After you've begun this journey of repentance, will you be willing to go even further, to share in that cup of suffering with Him? To delve into our dark past and drink from that same cup, to bear witness to what our Church forefathers have done, just as He has witnessed?

But once you begin, don't forget that this is only one side of the coin, for once He made that journey, He came out the other side, radiant in glory, changed forever. And as you embark on this journey of repentance, and drink of that cup to share in the fellowship of His suffering, you too will inevitably come through it, and be changed. Forever.

Will you pray this repentance prayer with me?

Heavenly Father,

We thank You for the invitation to fellowship with You in Your suffering. Even though this is a painful journey, one that begins with repentance, we acknowledge that it is a necessary journey, necessary if we are to see the breakthroughs in our personal lives we wish to see; necessary if we are to see the breakthroughs in the greater unfolding of Your plans on Earth in these last days; and necessary if we are to see Your people — both Jew and Christian — united in spirit.

We ask that Your people would ultimately forgive us for our history of antisemitism, even as You have forgiven us.

We also acknowledge that as we proceed along this journey of repentance, it will lead us to fellowship with You in Your suffering, which we desire to embrace with all our heart, and all our soul, and all our mind, and all our strength, knowing that it will deepen our relationship with You; knowing that we will be conformed to Your image in the process; and knowing that we will be forever changed as a result.

We open our hearts to allow You to do this work in us, for which we thank You LORD.

In Jesus' precious and glorious name,

Amen.

How I Began My Repentance Journey with The LIST

by Laura Densmore

I have a very precious group of women that I meet with on the phone each week. We gather four times per week on an early morning conference call to pray for one hour. On one of the days, we pray for our children and grandchildren. On another day, we pray over current events happening in Israel, and then pray scriptures over the nation. Last summer, our group became aware of The LIST that had been published on Root-Source.com.[1] We had each signed the petition[2], and then downloaded a PDF copy of The LIST.

We decided as a group that we would read through The LIST in advance of our call, and then have a "solemn assembly" repentance phone conference call on the 9th of Av (July 23rd, 2018) in the spirit of Joel 2:15-17:

> *"Blow the trumpet in Zion, sanctify a fast, call a solemn assembly: Gather the people, sanctify the congregation, assemble the elders, gather the children, and those that suck the breasts: let the bridegroom go forth of his chamber, and the bride out of her closet.*
>
> *Let the priests, the ministers of the LORD, weep between the porch and the altar, and let them say, Spare thy people, O LORD give not thine heritage to reproach, that the heathen should rule over them: wherefore should they say among the people, Where is their God?"* (KJV)

As the 9th of Av was approaching, I opened up The LIST to read through it; it took many hours. A heavy weight descended upon me, and the more I read, the heavier the weight became. I already knew of the Inquisitions, the Crusades, the Pogroms, and the Holocaust, but there was so much more that I didn't know.

For example, I had never even heard of ritual murder blood libels (*see entry on The LIST, 1247*). This entry details how in Valréas, France, a 2-year old child mysteriously died just before Passover. Because it happened near the time of Passover, this brought suspicion upon the Jews who were accused of killing the child. I quote from The LIST:

> "Three Jews were imprisoned and tortured, and confessed to the charges. More Jews were imprisoned and tortured, which led to Jews being quartered, burnt alive, men being castrated, and women having their breasts removed."

I let that one sink deep into my heart and the tears began to well up. It felt like a stone had been thrown into the pond of my soul. The waves kept rippling out and I was forever changed. A fountain of tears was opened up within me that I didn't know existed. In my secret place where I pray, I laid my head upon the shoulder of my Father and wept with Him. We cried.....together.

How could it be that our Church forefathers had done this to the Jews? How could I not have known about this?

On the solemn assembly phone call, we opened with the sounding of the shofar. Then, one by one, each woman shared one item from The LIST that had cut her heart, and after sharing, she prayed a prayer of repentance over that item.

Repentance is not something that can be "drummed up or manufactured". It is a gift from God. He is the One who sends the spirit of repentance upon us. If we have hearts to receive it, if we "catch" that spirit, then He can truly do a deep work within each one of us.

On that prayer call, I witnessed the spirit of repentance from God move very deeply upon each woman. The weeping came upon us. The tears flowed. The blindness fell away. We SAW. We SAW what our Church forefathers had done to the precious Jewish people, and we were broken and undone.

One of the ladies on the call prayed this prayer: *"Abba, this cannot stop here. More people in the Church need to know about The LIST. Would You call Your people to repent over the sins of our Church forefathers in a much wider way? This cannot stop here. There is more. Abba, please cause this go out to wider audience."*

We decided to meet again by phone to "debrief" from what the LORD had done in our hearts on the 9th of Av. I had recently met Bob O'Dell by phone and asked if he and co-author of The LIST, Ray Montgomery, would like to join us on this "debriefing" phone call.

Two weeks later, we had our "debriefing" phone conference call. Each woman shared briefly what reading through The LIST had done in her own heart, and how the repentance time together on the 9th of Av had affected her. After all had shared, Bob and Ray "weighed in" and shared their hearts with us.[3]

It was not long after that, that our team came up with the idea of writing the 40 Days of Repentance "Companion Guide" to The LIST. And so began my journey of walking in a lifestyle of repentance, especially concerning the sins of my Church forefathers. All contributors to this book are doing so in a volunteer capacity. After covering publication costs, any/all profits will accrue directly to Root Source as an act of repentance and restitution towards the Jewish people.

There is a biblical basis for repenting over the sins of our Church forefathers:

> *"If they shall confess their iniquity, **and the iniquity of their fathers**, with their trespass which they trespassed against me, and that also they have walked contrary unto me; And that I also have walked contrary unto them, and have brought them into the land of their enemies; if then their uncircumcised hearts be humbled, and they then accept the punishment of their iniquity: Then will I remember my covenant with Jacob, and also my covenant with Isaac, and also my covenant with Abraham will I remember; and I will remember the land."* LEVITICUS 26:40-42 (KJV, emphasis mine)

What is the "iniquity of their fathers"? I had always viewed this passage as a prayer for repenting of the generational sin in a family bloodline. I had always used it as a pattern of prayer for repenting of the sins of my literal father, my grandfather, and for repenting of specific sins in my own family bloodline. But the Holy Spirit revealed this passage to me in a new way and I saw it in a whole new light. There is another dimension to this "iniquity of the fathers," and it has to do with ***Repenting of the Sins of our "Church" Forefathers***.

What IS the sin of our "Church" forefathers? What The LIST did for me was to unveil and reveal the "sins of our Church fathers" in a way that allowed me to come to my own conclusions, and to respond to the LORD directly.

Reading through The LIST can be likened to this: it is like I have been attending a familiar and well-loved church for a long time, but then I discover a staircase leading down to a basement. I didn't know there was a basement in my church? I walk down the stairs to the basement, but it is pitch black down there. What should I do? I could just go back upstairs and "ignore" the basement. Instead, I look for and then find the light switch (that is, I read The LIST), the light turns on and now the room is filled with light. *It is a chamber of horrors and torture used against the Jewish people.* In MY basement. Of MY church. It is now between me and the LORD for me to decide what I will do about this.

Reading through The LIST opened MY blind eyes to see things I had never seen before. I could not read it all at once. I would read for a while, absorb the weight of it, allow what I had just read to break my heart, pray prayers of repentance, take a break, and then come back to it.

It is my conviction that we must "own" the sins of our Church forefathers, and then repent of these iniquities. This is vital in order to heal the breach between Jews and Christians.

Will you pray this repentance prayer with me?

Abba,

Truly we have been so blind, so self absorbed, so full of our own self-righteousness and pride. Abba, thank You for beginning to open our eyes to SEE the sins of our Church forefathers. It is not pretty. It is horrific. Abba, we prostrate ourselves before You. We now own these sins of our Church forefathers. Abba, would You have mercy upon us? We are asking You to forgive us for these heinous crimes, murders and persecutions done against Your people, the Jews. Abba, would You open the sealed-up fountain of tears within us and allow those tears to flow?

We weep with You, Abba, to read of these things. May our tears begin to bring healing to hearts, and to somehow heal the breach. Would You please remove the plank of pride out of our eyes? Abba, would You somehow use that plank to build a bridge between Christians and Jews so we can approach our Jewish brethren in humility, in love and in service?

In Yeshua's name,

Amen.

ENDNOTES:

1. https://root-source.com/blog/9av-resources-post/
2. https://root-source.com/will-you-do-this-towards-reconciliation-between-christians-and-jews/
3. https://soundcloud.com/user-552350389/discussion_the-list_8918

For What Do We Do This?

by Bob O'Dell

B y reading this book you are part of a collective act of repentance. And because we are doing it together, we can, in a certain sense, refer to it using the word: ceremony. God invented ceremony when He invented the *Passover*. And when God instituted that Passover ceremony for the fledgling nation of Israel, He anticipated that the next generation would ask to know the reason for keeping the Passover.

> *"And when your children ask you, 'What does this ceremony mean to you?' then tell them..."* EXODUS 12:26-27A (NIV)

We can apply that very question to *our* 40-day-long ceremony, especially in light of the vile nature of this history of events that are chronicled in The LIST. For instance, The LIST records the following dates for certain "firsts", a few of which are listed below:

- First Anti-Jewish restriction of activities: 132 CE
- First Anti-Jewish Writing by a Christian Forefather: 155 CE
- First Pogrom led by a Christian Forefather: 414 CE
- First recorded killing in the name of Christ: 547 CE
- First Expulsion perpetrated by Christians: 561 CE
- First Blood Libel: 1144 CE
- First Desecration of the Host: 1243 CE

Now let's be honest with ourselves. As authors of this project we have gathered and documented lists of evil acts, documenting the downward spiral of mankind! The Apostle Paul describes the evil "firsts" just listed above when, at the end of Romans 1, he writes:

> *"slanderers, God-haters, insolent, arrogant and boastful; **they invent ways** **of doing evil**; they disobey their parents;"* ROMANS 1:30 (NIV, emphasis mine)

The LIST documents many forms of evil that were invented by men! Is it right to document such things? The question is reasonable! Consider what Paul says in his letter to the Philippians:

> *"Finally, brothers and sisters, whatever is true, whatever is noble, whatever is right, whatever is pure, whatever is lovely, whatever is admirable—if anything is excellent or praiseworthy—think about such things."* PHILIPPIANS 4:8 (NIV)

Paul commands us to absorb our minds in that which is good rather than evil. Then what, pray tell, are we doing spending time to understand evil acts? What shall we answer to our children when they ask the reason?

I would like to propose three reasons.

Reason 1: TO INCREASE OUR FAITH

When I look at the truth of how we as the Church have correctly seen Jesus as Savior, and yet have been so mired and bogged down in Replacement Theology, I marvel — not in disillusionment, but at the greatness of God. How is it that we as a Church could have embarked on a downward spiral such as we have, and God has not disowned us and cut us off along the way? How is it that we could invent new ways to do evil, and yet God still considers us His children through that amazing and massive finished work of Jesus Christ on the Cross?

Viewing the historical truth of this LIST, I believe, allows us to increase our faith in a God who does not back down on His *New Covenant* promise to us. Similarly, viewing the re-establishment of the State of Israel in our days allows us to have our faith increased in a God who does not back down on His *Everlasting Covenant* promises to Israel.

For what do we do this "ceremony" of repentance? We do it for faith.

Reason 2: TO INCREASE OUR HOPE

When I look at the downward spiral of separation and replacement of the Jewish people by the Church through the ages, I see that throughout history a few Christians are recorded as refusing to separate themselves emotionally or physically from their fellow Jews. About this, I marvel at the story that God is writing in the Christian world.

Consider the stories of:

1. Pope Urban V, who protected Jews from forced baptisms in the year 1365 CE.

2. Oliver Cromwell, who led the fight to allow Jews to return to England in the year 1655 CE.

3. Johann Ignaz von Dollinger, who was excommunicated for standing against improper use of power by the Church and against antisemitism in the year 1871 CE.

God was always writing, and is writing in an ever increasing way, a story of hope for the future. And now we have the blessed opportunity to become part of that very story of hope, to be part of an acceleration of the move of God on the earth.

Ultimately, viewing The LIST increases my hope that we ARE, and WILL ultimately prepare the way of the coming of the LORD. It is the greatest of valleys that makes the greatest of mountains so glorious in comparison. The destination is sure.

For what do we do this "ceremony" of repentance? We do it for hope.

Reason 3: FOR LOVE

On the 9th of Av in 2013, I discovered the truth of what was lurking in my own heart: that I carried arrogance against the Jewish people because "I had Jesus living in my heart and they did not". I marvelled: how could I not have known this history? Why had I never been taught these things? Why were we hiding this historical truth from ourselves? I felt broken and undone.

But while I carried this sense of brokenness in the months that followed, something beautiful happened much more quickly than I would have imagined. Our family had previously planned a vacation in Israel that summer, and so a mere two weeks after the 9th of Av, I found myself in Israel, not for business purposes as I had come the past thirty times prior, but just for enjoyment. What I am about to tell you never happened to me in the thirty prior visits, nor in the twenty visits since. On that one visit alone, I was asked by random Israeli Jews looking right at me, probably close to a dozen times:

"First time in Israel?"

I answered truthfully, "No", on every single occasion!

And in one of those encounters, two Jewish men, after having opened with that very question while I was gazing out at Mount Zion, concluded our brief conversation with the words:

"Welcome to Jerusalem!"

What was all this about? Do I believe that God now loved me more because I was repenting of our horrible past? Absolutely not!

But do I believe that because I had taken upon myself some inkling of my arrogance and the sins of my forefathers, **that I myself loved God more?** Absolutely yes!

> *"For this reason I say to you, her sins, which are many, have been forgiven, for she loved much; but he who is forgiven little, loves little."* LUKE 7:47 (NASB)

There was in that process of repentance, a turning of myself towards God. Not only did I love God more, but I was able to receive God's love to me more fully. Of course I wasn't loved more — how could I be — but I was now able to receive it.

By the question those Israelis asked me throughout that 10 day vacation in Israel, I can see now that God was indicating His forgiveness to me. In addition, I was receiving His love through the asking of that question.

Was it my first time in Israel? Apparently the answer was: "Yes, it was." And with that understanding I can now speak with all confidence.

For what do we do this "ceremony" of repentance? We do it for love.

In Summary

The Apostle Paul sums up our life before God very simply in 1 Corinthians, when he concludes one of the greatest chapters in the entire Bible with these words:

> *"And now these three remain: faith, hope and love. But the greatest of these is love."* 1 CORINTHIANS 13:13 (NIV)

Will you pray this repentance prayer with me?

Father in Heaven,

As we walk along this 40-day path of repentance, would You align our hearts towards You and Your purposes? Would You increase our faith in who You are, and Your greatness? Would You increase our faith in Your steadfast keeping of covenant towards Christians and Jews?

Would You profoundly increase our hope in Your plans and purposes going forward? Will You undergird our hearts with an unflinching resolve that Your story is still being written? Will You give us eyes to see remnants of good in the midst of the bad, and strengthen our faith to do our part to prepare the coming of Your kingdom so that Your kingdom will come on earth as it is in heaven?

Finally, would You allow us to grow in our love towards You in this process? You proclaim that those who are forgiven little will love little. Then let us move in the other direction! Would You reveal to us, by Your Spirit, the places in our hearts that still need confession and forgiveness, and in so doing, would You allow us to love You more and more in the process?

And finally, in Your perfect way and in Your perfect timing would You allow us to receive from You the incomprehensible, life changing experience of Your love for us? We can only love You because You first loved us! You are the great initiator of love! Allow us the joy of knowing and experiencing Your great love for us.

In Yeshua's name, we pray.

Amen.

Cornelius — A Gentile Stone

by Bob O'Dell

The very fact that The LIST had to be compiled at all, shows that something went very, very wrong in the history of the Church. But did it go wrong right at the very beginning of Church history or not?

Peter, a Jew, was given the honor of having his name declared to him by Jesus in the very same verse in which Jesus promised to establish the Church. He declared *"...you are Peter, and on this rock I will build my Church...".* (Matthew 16:18 NIV)

And it was this very Peter, who later would personally witness the honor given to Cornelius, when the Holy Spirit would fall upon Cornelius and all his household, recalling the amazing events of Acts 2 that occurred seven years earlier in Jerusalem. If the Church was born on Pentecost Sunday among Jews in Jerusalem, it was *extended* seven years later among Gentiles in the coastal town of Caesarea.

God specifically chose and affirmed Cornelius. Therefore, he must have exhibited behaviors that would be **helpful** in the **proper** building of the Church. And yet, why do we in the Church today not tell his full story, the full story that Luke took great efforts to describe for us in Acts Chapter 10? Perhaps you might choose to stop and read that chapter right now before continuing.

What specifically, can we learn from Cornelius, this first gentile stone that was being fitted into the faith in Jesus/Yeshua in 40 CE, as mentioned in The LIST?

Pictured above: Cornelius, one of the first "gentile stones"

First, the story of Cornelius does not occur in Rome, nor in any of the "nations", but right there in Israel, on the coastline. Yes, Caesarea was a Roman city, with all the pagan trappings of such a city, but yet it WAS in Israel. The lesson I take from this is that God's blessing is available for Christians who visit THE LAND of Israel, who are willing to spend any amount of time there.

Second, Cornelius' job required him to take an oath of loyalty to Caesar. Not only that, he arrived to Israel from Rome of all places, the center of antagonism towards the Jews. Is it not just like God to choose someone from the *most unlikely* place? Do you feel like your own history makes you unlikely to be used by God in helping bridge the divide between the Church and the Jews? Think again! It is in God's nature to use the unlikely.

Third, the passage clearly tells us that Cornelius gave alms to the Jewish people in Israel, and that this giving had been favorably noticed by God. Cornelius was blessing Israel! Then God bestowed upon him more honor and blessing than he ever expected. Imagine if that idea had been taught continuously over the last 2,000 years—what a difference it would have made in Church history!

Fourth, the passage strongly implies that Cornelius did his giving of alms in RELATIONSHIP to the Jewish people. It was not subservient relationship, and neither was it authoritarian control, but peer relationship built around love. Where this love came from and how it began, we do not know, but we do know from the text that Cornelius was God-fearing and devout. Perhaps the message of the text is that one way for us to assess the quality of our vertical relationship with God, is to examine the quality of our horizontal relationships with those around us — those with whom we would not necessarily expect to have relationship. Today, even if not a single Jew lives in your town, in this age of the Internet, it is now possible to step into relationship with Jews anywhere in the world.

And lastly, let us examine the moment in which the story of Cornelius transitioned from the natural, to the supernatural:

> *"About the ninth hour of the day he clearly saw in a vision an angel of God who had just come in and said to him, 'Cornelius!'. And fixing his gaze on him and being much alarmed, he said, 'What is it, Lord?' And he said to him, 'Your prayers and alms have ascended as a memorial before God.'"* Acts 10:3-4 (NASB)

Do you want to be overwhelmed by the favor of God, and to have supernatural visions and visitations from God? Many Christian books tell stories and give advice about how a person can position themselves to experience the presence of God in a stronger way. But in this case, God clearly explains that He has been touched by his prayer and his alms to the Jewish people. Has anyone ever suggested to you before this moment, that perhaps a way for YOU to position yourself to receive amazing visions and prophetic revelation from God, is to first step into proper relationship with the Jews?

This idea did not first come to me from Acts 10, although I wish I had had eyes to read it that way. It came to mind first, after we invited a few Christians to our home for a meeting to discuss ideas for how we might do more for Israel and the Jews. Within the first ten minutes at the lunch table, right after we asked God's blessing over the food, two people got healed in quick succession. I began to think about whether God might be signaling that His power is more readily available to us when we align in purpose towards Israel and the Jews. Only after that experience did I notice that principle was plainly seen in this passage!

Peter only stayed a few days with Cornelius. What would Cornelius have done next? Would he have walked away from his Jewish relationships, now that he believed that Jesus was the Messiah? The text is silent on this, and on everything that happened afterward.

But, may I ask you the question? Imagine YOU had just been visited by an angel and YOU had been told that your prayers and alms had ascended as a memorial before God. Would that make you more likely, or less likely to continue doing those things that brought about the vision in the first place? Even though

Cornelius now believed that Jesus was the Messiah, can you possibly even imagine that Cornelius would have STOPPED those actions after the Holy Spirit fell upon him? I find it inconceivable that he would stop. If anything, he would do it all the more!

Clearly God has always desired that the Church walk in relationship with the Jews. Yes, we walked away, but that was our own fault. God's plan in Acts chapter 10 was clear. We just had to read it, and see it as a pattern for ourselves.

Cornelius was a gentile stone, the first of its kind to be fitted into the church. May we fully learn that lesson.

Will you pray this repentance prayer with me?

Father in Heaven,

Thank You for choosing the Roman Gentile Cornelius to be the first gentile Christian. Thank You for showing us a clear model in scripture for travelling to Israel, for choosing the most unlikely people, for finding tangible ways to bless Israel, including our money and our time, for encouraging us to walk in relationship with the Jews around us, and to believe that Your power will not be absent from our lives, when we do so.

But Father, please forgive our Church forefathers for not passing down to us the idea of reading Cornelius, not just as a special case in world history, but as a beautiful gentile stone that You had placed into the spiritual house You were building. Forgive us today for not seeing Cornelius as a gentile stone to which we can be fitted and joined.

Forgive us for separating ourselves from the Jewish people. Forgive us and our Church forefathers for finding excuses to walk away from relationship. Forgive us and our forefathers for focusing on their imperfections and faults rather than focusing on ways to walk as a blessing to the Jewish people. Forgive us for hardening our hearts. Indeed, reach down into the hearts of each one of us, and replace our hearts of stone with hearts of flesh — and if that flesh You give us was ever so much like that flesh that was within the very first gentile believer, Cornelius, then we would be ever so eternally grateful.

In Yeshua's name, we pray.

Amen.

The Second Temple: Never a Second Thought

by Bob O'Dell

Have you ever shed even one tear over the fall of the Roman Empire? Or the Babylonian Empire?

Ever felt a bit down when you thought about the Persian Empire being overthrown by the Greeks, or when the Greeks succumbed to the rule of the Romans?

Have you ever looked at the ruins of a great amphitheater or stadium and then sat down, put your head in your hands and cried?

If you have, you are a member of a club that I have never joined. To me these events are simply history. I have hardly given these things a second thought. They do not move me at all.

But, I would submit to you that both you and I have missed something. Something important. Something that is actually worth crying about, even though I never gave it a second thought — the burning and destruction of Jerusalem and the Second Temple.

As The LIST points out, this event took place in 70 CE and is described as follows:

> *"The second Temple is destroyed by Titus after a siege that began in 66 CE. Josephus also records that 97,000 Jews were sold as slaves. The population went from 600,000 before the siege to between around 40,000 after."*

Pictured above: The destruction of the Second Temple in 70 AD.

The question I would like to ask you to consider today is:

How do you feel about that event?

The writings of the Church fathers mentioned in The LIST from 70 CE onwards allow us to deduce their answers to that question. In today's language we might express them as:

Good riddance.

Had it coming to them.

Hurray! They finally reaped what they sowed!

Christ killers!

Should have taken Jesus at His word!

But may I suggest an even more important question might be:

How might God and Christ have felt about those events?

Such questions first came up for me when I was speaking with my friend Steve Hawthorne in 2018 about what sort of prayers we Christians could pray alongside the Jews on the 9th of Av. Steve jolted me (without knowing it) when he said "if we as Christians truly believe that we are grafted into Abraham, and

Israel, then we should be grieving the loss of the Second Temple right along with the Jews". He jolted me again when he said, "The first century Christians would have been emotionally heartbroken at its destruction."

I had never thought of that. I had never once given the fall of the Second Temple a second thought! This, I thought, was a "Jewish problem". Since I was not Jewish, it just didn't pertain to me.

But, what was the situation on the occasion when Jesus said those famous words:

> *"And He said to them, 'Do you not see all these things? Truly I say to you, not one stone here will be left upon another, which will not be torn down.'"*
> MATTHEW 24:2 (NASB)

Was he railing against the Pharisees with outstretched arm and pointed finger? No, while it is true He was outside, He was speaking with His disciples who were pointing out its buildings.

While it is absolutely possible to connect "Jesus' not being recognized by His own people" to "the destruction of the Second Temple 38 years later", we must also consider if speaking those words gave him joy. The Temple plan was given to Moses in God's presence. Its purpose was to be a place on earth where God meets with man. How could the destruction of that Temple be, to God, an act of good riddance? Allow me to amplify that question. How could the destruction of the Temple, whose very plan was given to Moses in God's presence, whose purpose was to be a place on earth where God meets man, how could the destruction of that Temple be to God, an act of good riddance?

The prophets never claimed that God limited Himself to reside in a Temple, even when the Temple stood tall in Jerusalem (Isaiah 66:1). It is true that Jesus also told Pilate *"My kingdom is not of this world"* (John 18:36). But did that mean that because Jesus was heavenly minded he was against all earthly good?

The Jews have recorded that while the Temple was in operation, and while sacrifices were being made, that there was no stench, no unpleasant odor, and no flies. The smell was sweet.

Today, many could consider that animal sacrifices are abusive to animals. No way! Today, Christians have been taught to believe that Jews consider animal sacrifice as a formula for the forgiveness of sins. No way! The Jews knew that only God can forgive sins, especially those of outright rebellion and iniquity.

Consider the fruit of the Temple's destruction. Did the destruction of the Second Temple bring glory to God's name among the nations? No.

Instead, our Church forefathers used the debacle of the Second Temple, and the expulsion of most of the Jews from Jerusalem, as "clear evidence that God has left his Jewish people". It was the strongest fact yet, that could be suggested as evidence for Replacement Theology — that God had shifted His covenant promises, His favor, His blessing away from Israel to the Church.

Our forefathers would take up that "evidence" from the dust of that city, and throw it onto the downtrodden heads of countless Jews for exactly 1,897 years, until 1967, when Jerusalem would once again come under full Jewish control!

On the contrary, the early Christians were not opposed to the Temple. They met at or near the Temple often. Christian leadership was centered in Jerusalem. And finally, when Jerusalem was surrounded, the Christians, having read the prophecies of Jesus in the book of Luke, left for what is now Petra in Jordan. But to even consider that they would rejoice at the destruction of the Temple and of the city is ludicrous. Their own extended Jewish families and friends would certainly have been affected.

The early Christians in Jerusalem, the vast majority being of Jewish descent, would have considered the loss of the Second Temple and the destruction of Jerusalem to be a time of great lament. And in a turn of events beyond all coincidence, the significance of that destruction was signaled in its timing! The First Temple and the Second Temple were both destroyed on the SAME day, the 9th of Av.

Yet, in the midst of that pain, was the promise — for God had previously said through the prophet Zechariah, that eventually the fast day of the 9th of Av, would become a feast day — a day of great rejoicing for all Jews. Therefore, the timing of the destruction of the Second Temple showed that this would not be the last word in Jewish history. An even greater promise of something still to come, would greatly outweigh even this absolute catastrophe. The promise would be a reformed kingdom, a rebuilt Temple, and a coming Messiah who rules from Jerusalem! (Isaiah 2:1-4, Revelation 21:2-3, Ezekiel 41:1 & 43:4-5).

These hopes were never forgotten by the Jews. If we had only stopped to listen to the heart of God, we might have actually given the Second Temple more than just a second thought, and we might have learned that its destruction was signalling not God's replacement, but God's promise.

Will you pray this repentance prayer with me?

Father in Heaven,

We in our own small ways have lost sight of what it was like for our earliest Church forefathers to stand by and watch that great destruction come upon Jerusalem and the Second Temple. We have rarely considered what it might be like for YOU to look down from heaven and see Your own plans go up in flames. We have rarely considered the insults defaming Your power and Your character that were sent Your way by all the nations who hated the Jews, and the One true God of Israel.

Father, forgive us for our thoughtlessness. Forgive us for thinking about the loss of the Second Temple as a loss for Jews, and a gain for ourselves. Forgive us for not considering ourselves to be grafted into that very Kingdom called Israel, and receiving upon ourselves the shame of that destruction as the nations railed against you.

Forgive us for thinking in terms of "us and them". Of winners and losers. Of Christians versus Jews. Forgive us as Christians for taking advantage of this loss, and using it against Your people the Jews. Forgive us for taking to ourselves the good promises, and placing upon the Jews just the destruction and burning, as if this destruction brought You no pain.

Give us eyes to see the Temple the way You see it. And if and when You, in Your great glory, allow the Jews to rebuild a Third Temple, then begin to prepare our hearts to come into perfect alignment with Your plans and purposes for a Third Temple, even as we eagerly await the return of Jesus the Messiah.

In Yeshua's name, we pray.

Amen.

Repenting for the Sins of Our Church Fathers Towards the Jews

by Jeff Daly

"Then they said to one another, 'Come, let us make bricks and bake them thoroughly.' They had brick for stone, and they had asphalt for mortar. And they said, 'Come, let us build ourselves a city, and a tower whose top is in the heavens; let us make a name for ourselves, lest we be scattered abroad over the face of the whole earth.'" GENESIS 11:3-4 (NKJV)

The pride of the human heart without the Living God will build a palace to self and tear down that which is Holy.

It all began when Titus destroyed the Second Temple on the 9th of Av in 70 CE (*see entries on the LIST for all these 9th of Av events: 70, 71, 130 and 135*).

A year later, in 71 CE, and also on the 9th of Av, the Romans plowed Jerusalem over with salt to destroy any vegetation necessary that would support a population. This turned the city into a Roman colony totally dependent on Rome for survival, thus fulfilling Micah 3:12:

"Therefore because of you, Zion will be plowed like a field, Jerusalem will become a heap of rubble, the temple hill a mound overgrown with thickets." (NIV)

In 130 CE, again on the 9th of Av, Roman Emperor Hadrian ordered Governor Rufus to plow Jerusalem over in preparation for building a new pagan city, Aelia Capitolina, on the location.

Six years later, in 136 CE - and once again on the 9th of Av - Jerusalem was rebuilt as the Roman city of Aelia Capitolina, the region of "Israel" was changed to "Palaestina", and pagan Rome exalted itself in building a heathen temple to Jupiter on the Temple site in Jerusalem.

Example of a Roman Temple that would have been built in place of the Jewish Holy Temple.

What were the followers of Yeshua the Messiah doing as this happened? Did a Holy Spirit-filled leader like Stephen come forward to witness for Christ and attempt to stop this blasphemy? As Jerusalem was again paganized and as the Romans changed the region of "Israel" to "Palaestina", had antisemitism set in even deeper?

Pride infects all of us. Until we repent and remove that wicked stronghold out of our hearts with the conviction of the Holy Spirit and God's Holy Word, we act as if we don't need God. Apart from the Living God we focus on flesh, family, fame, fortune, and fear of others instead of fear of God.

Focusing on self, we abandon His Chosen People, and His Eternal Plan of Redemption through the God of Abraham, Isaac, Jacob and Yeshua the Messiah.

Here is a question to ponder: if you and I were among the believers in Yeshua in Jerusalem in 136 CE, would we have had the courage to stand for His Temple in the face of paganism? To stand for Jews and the Hebrew roots of our faith, even in the face of death? Would we have had the Holy Spirit fruit of faith to stand for the Truth of His Word and to come alongside Jewish believers to protect them and the Temple site?

You and I today face the same choice and decision. Paganism abounds in the church today. Church leaders today are often lukewarm. There is a willingness to go along with the culture to make services "seeker friendly." Roman secularism has again raised itself up as the culture declines. Few know the Living God.

You and I are the temple of the Holy Spirit, as it is written in 1 Corinthians 6:19:

> *"Or do you not know that your body is a temple of the Holy Spirit who is in you, whom you have from God, and that you are not your own?"* (NASB)

This priceless gift is from the Living God. We are not our own.

So this very day we face the same choice as did church leaders in Jerusalem in 136 CE. Will we be courageous in the face of pagan attacks? Will our temples be paganized?

The Risen Christ tells us that "the cowardly" are the first group not to be allowed into heaven, as it is written in Revelation 21:8:

> *"But the cowardly, unbelieving, abominable, murderers, sexually immoral, sorcerers, idolaters, and all liars shall have their part in the lake which burns with fire and brimstone, which is the second death."* (NKJV)

We honor Yeshua by bowing before His Holy Name as we preserve and cleanse our Holy Spirit temples.

The lesson we should take from this is that you and I are not to build a "palace to Self."

Will you pray this repentance prayer with me?

Abba Father,

In Yeshua's Holy Name, I repent for the sins of my ancestors in failing to protect Jews and the Hebrew roots of our faith. Please forgive me for my pride. Forgive me for any cowardice to confront others who would tear down Your Truth. Forgive me for not standing up for Israel and for our Jewish brothers and sisters as they face persecution.

> *"Create in me a clean heart, O God, and renew a steadfast spirit within me."* (PSALM 51:10, NASB)

In Yeshua's Holy, Holy Name, the Name above all names.

Amen and Amen.

Marcion's Heresy and Us

by Bob O'Dell

One of the most infamous heretics in early Christian history was Marcion of Sinope, who finds some of his thoughts expressed in The LIST in the year 140 CE. This Marcion, also referred to as Marcion of Pontus, taught that which became known as the Gospel of Marcion, which took hold in many churches in Asia.

He believed that the "God" described by Jesus and Paul was not the same "God" that was described in the Hebrew scriptures. In other words, the "God" of the New Testament, was not actually the same "God" as described in the Old Testament. He even edited some of the writings of (what became) the New Testament to remove passages with which he did not agree.

Pictured above: Marcion of Sinope.

Wikipedia summarizes his teachings in this way:

> *"Study of the Hebrew Scriptures, along with received writings circulating in the nascent Church, led Marcion to conclude that many of the teachings of Jesus were incompatible with the actions of Yahweh, the belligerent god of the Hebrew Bible. Marcion responded by developing a ditheistic system of belief around the year 144."*[1]

A ditheistic system is a dualistic view that allows two fundamentally different aspects to coexist simultaneously. In Marcion's view, this was the benevolent God of the New Testament and the malevolent God of the Old Testament.

Marcion Referenced Paul

Paul had died more than seventy years earlier. Had he been living, he certainly would have opposed Marcion. Even more so, it was Marcion's decision to base much of his proposed theology on some of Paul's letters, or modified versions thereof, which would have been an especially cruel blow to Paul.

Paul must have had in mind the boldness of persons such as Marcion when he wrote to the Ephesians:

> *"I know that after my departure savage wolves will come in among you, not sparing the flock; and from among your own selves men will arise, speaking perverse things, to draw away the disciples after them."* ACTS 20:29-30 (NASB)

Marcion was one such savage wolf. Many disciples were drawn away. About this there can be no argument.

Marcion spoke heresy.

And What of Us Today?

While his followers were known as Marcionites, when viewed from those outside of Christianity, his views were close enough to Christian orthodoxy that his followers were referred to as Christians. In fact, in those early days, and without a formal agreement on the contents and correct versions of the New Testament canon, there was no way to contain and control which of his beliefs would take hold within the Christian community.

Marcion's beliefs spread.

Not only did some of Marcion's beliefs take hold, but some of Marcion's beliefs persist today.

Today, the heresy of Marcion has found its place within our churches in a slightly muted form. We don't believe that the God of the New Testament and the God of the Old Testament were actually different "God's", but we see God as acting with more malevolence in the Old Testament than in the New Testament. We even refer to the Age of Law versus the Age of Grace (also known as "Dispensationalism"). We also refer to the New Testament as the Gospel, or "Good News", leaving hearers to infer that the Hebrew Scriptures are therefore the "bad news".

I am not ashamed of the Gospel for it is the power of God unto salvation, but I am not ashamed of the Hebrew Scriptures either!

A Larger Work

I believe that God has a work He wants to do in the Church. God wants us to eradicate from our midst the remaining strains of (un)belief that in former times unleashed atrocities against the Jews. More positively, God wants to help us grow into a larger perspective of the Hebrew scriptures.

Is the Old Testament really to be thought of as old, or is it to be thought of as *first*?

Are the Old Testaments and New Testaments two *different* Testaments, or do they contain one integrated message of mercy from the One True God who says He does not change?

> *"For I am the LORD, I change not."* MALACHI 3:6 (KJV)

> *"But the mercy of the LORD is from everlasting to everlasting upon them that fear him, and his righteousness unto children's children;"* PSALMS 103:17 (KJV)

We do **not** need to agree on what all these things mean. We do **not** have to have a common theology to repent for the sins of the past. We only have to have a willingness to step in and repent.

All I am saying is, I don't think the work of repentance, and the need for repentance regarding the Jews, will be complete until we have come into full alignment with how God sees the Hebrew scriptures and the Greek scriptures.

Without knowing what full alignment with God looks like, we can at least agree to pray that God would, in His mercy, help us in the journey and open our eyes to "see" that to which we are still blind.

And for Marcion himself, I can't help but wonder how the world would be a different place today if he had heeded the words of James, the brother of Jesus who said flatly:

> *"Let not many of you become teachers..."* JAMES 3:1 (NASB)

Will you pray this repentance prayer with me?

Father in Heaven,

We thank You for the gathering together of the writings in the first century that resulted in those books that we today refer to as "The New Testament". We thank You that when Paul wrote "all scripture is inspired by God", only the Old Testament existed, so we have always been encouraged to accept the Old Testament as Your truth.

Please forgive us for that which we believe about You that is not in alignment with You. We do not walk in the fulness of understanding of who You are as Father, and in fullness of understanding of Jesus, the Messiah. Our prayer today is that we might come into better understanding of You as a God who does not change. Our prayer today is that we might also come into better understanding of You as a God whose mercy extends from everlasting to everlasting to those who fear Him.

We ask You to weed out and remove from our midst all unrighteousness that still remains, being seeded into our midst from the teachings of Marcion and all others involved. Restore to the church today the fullness of understanding that was embodied in Christ and the teachings of the New Testament, and show us how those thoughts are fully embodied in the Hebrew Scriptures as well.

And may Your will be done regarding the terms "Old and New Testaments" which we currently use.

In Yeshua's name, we pray.

Amen.

ENDNOTES:

1. https://en.wikipedia.org/wiki/Marcion_of_Sinope

A First Century Conversation Between a Christian and a Jew: Justin Martyr and Trypho

by Laura Densmore

Justin Martyr is heralded as one of the early founding Church forefathers. He is found on The LIST in the year 155-160 CE.

In the "Dialogue with Trypho", Justin Martyr[1] seeks to convince Trypho, who is Jewish, that Jesus is the Messiah. The dialogue contains many arguments which have become central to the Replacement Theology mindset. Trypho is not a real Jew, but a character Justin Martyr created so as to defeat him soundly. What Trypho says is Martyr's perception of what the Jews might think, believe, or say.

In reading selected portions of this dialogue (below), we can get a view through the "window" of time into what early Christian-Jewish relations were like back in the first century. In this essay,[2] Justin is having a conversation with Trypho (*emphases mine*):

CHAPTER X — TRYPHO BLAMES THE CHRISTIANS FOR THIS ALONE — THE NON-OBSERVANCE OF THE LAW (THE TORAH):

Pictured above: Justin Martyr.

"And when they ceased, I again addressed them thus:—

Justin Martyr:

> *Is there any other matter, my friends, in which we are blamed, than this, that we live not after the law (Torah), and are not circumcised in the flesh as your forefathers were, and do not observe Sabbaths as you do? Are our lives and customs also slandered among you?*

Trypho:

> *But this is what we are most at a loss about: that you, professing to be pious, and **supposing yourselves better than others**, are not in any particular separated from them, and do not alter your mode of living from the nations, in that **you observe no festivals or Sabbaths**, and do not have the rite of circumcision; and further, resting your hopes on a man that was crucified, you yet expect to obtain some good thing from God, **while you do not obey His commandments**.*
>
> *Have you not read, that soul shall be cut off from his people who shall not have been circumcised on the eighth day? And this has been ordained for strangers and for slaves equally. But you, **despising this covenant rashly**, reject the consequent duties, and attempt to persuade yourselves that you know God, when, however, you perform none of those things which they do who fear God. If, therefore, you can defend yourself on these points, and make it manifest in what way you hope for anything whatsoever, **even though you do not observe the law (Torah)**, this we would very gladly hear from you, and we shall make other similar investigations."*

What are Trypho's objections to the Christian faith?

To better understand the mindset that Trypho represents, to help frame the issues being discussed between them, and to follow the thread of Trypho's objections, allow me to share a definition for the Hebrew scriptures (the Old Testament) that you may not have encountered before:

> *Remember His **covenant** forever,*
> *The word which He commanded, for a thousand generations,*
> *The **covenant** which He made with Abraham, And His oath to Isaac,*
> *And confirmed it to Jacob for a statute,*
> *To Israel for an **everlasting covenant**.*
> 1 CHRONICLES 16:15-17 (NKJV, emphasis mine)

> *Therefore know that the Lord your God, He is God, the faithful God **who keeps covenant** and mercy for a thousand generations with those who love*

*Him and **keep His commandments;*** DEUTERONOMY 7:9 (NKJV, emphasis mine)

*They did not keep the **covenant** of God;*
They refused to walk in His law (Torah). PSALM 78:10 (NKJV, emphasis mine)

*"They kept not the **covenant** of God, and refused to **walk in His law (Torah).***" PSALM 78:10 (KJV, emphases mine)

In the world view that Trypho represents, the Torah, (that is, the Hebrew scriptures) IS the covenant between God and His people. He understood that when we keep His commands, we are stepping into God's covenant that He made with Abraham, Isaac, Jacob and Moses.

Conversely, if we don't follow His commands, then we are out of covenant with the God of Israel. The Torah is a covenant that God gave to His people, and to be in that covenant, we are to follow the Torah.

Let us return to the discussion between Justin Martyr and Trypho. Trypho's objections are the following:

1. You say you follow the God of Israel, but why do you not follow His Torah?

2. Following the Torah is stepping into the covenant that He made with us at Mt. Sinai, yet you do not follow the Torah (the law)? You seem to DESPISE the covenant He made with His people?

Justin replies to Trypho as follows:

CHAPTER XI — THE LAW ABROGATED; THE NEW TESTAMENT PROMISED AND GIVEN BY GOD.

*"But we do not trust through Moses or through the law; For the law promulgated on Horeb is **now old**, and belongs to yourselves alone; but this is for all universally. Now, law placed against law has abrogated that which is before it, and a covenant which comes after in like manner has put an end to the previous one; **and an eternal and final law—namely, Christ—**has been given to us, and the covenant is trustworthy, after which there **shall be no law, no commandment, no ordinance.***"

In Chapter 43, he concludes that the Law (the Torah) has ended and Christ replaces the Torah.

Reading this dialogue allows us to glean some important takeaways. Justin Martyr laid down a plank in the foundation of Replacement Theology when he stated that there is no law, no Torah, no commandment and no ordinance. Justin is saying that the Torah given to Moses at Mt. Sinai, God's commands and statutes, have been done away with and replaced by Christ.

I believe such thinking comes from a problem in our hearts. There was never a problem with the Torah (the Old Testament or the Hebrew scriptures). The problem was with our hearts:

> *"For finding fault **with them**, he says, Behold, the days come, says the LORD, when I will make **a new covenant** with the house of Israel and with the house of Judah: not according to the covenant that I made with their fathers in the day when I took them by the hand to lead them out of the land of Egypt; because they **continued not in my covenant**, and I regarded them not, says the LORD.*
>
> *For this is the **covenant** that I will make with the house of Israel after those days, says the LORD; I will put my laws (Torah) into their mind, and write it **in their hearts**: and I will be to them a God, and they shall be to me a people."*
> *Hebrews 8:8-10* (KJV, emphases mine)

A stony heart rejects the Torah, as it is written:

> *"Yea, they made their hearts as an adamant stone, lest they should hear the law (Torah), and the words which the LORD of hosts has sent in his spirit by the former prophets: therefore came a great wrath from the LORD of hosts."*
> ZECHARIAH 7:12 (KJV)

When the Old Testament is rejected due to stony hearts, this leads to the Replacement Theology mindset. In believing this doctrinal lie, a foundation was laid over the centuries which provided the structure for the scaffolding, walls, and roof in building the early Church. Little did we know that while the early Church was being constructed with planks of Replacement Theology, this resulted in the Church having a dark basement below filled with a chamber of horrors and tortures against the Jewish people (*see Devotion: How I Began My Repentance Journey with The LIST*).

Truly we have much blood upon our hands. Where do we even begin to repent? Perhaps if enough of us journey down the road of repentance for the sins of our Church forefathers, we can collectively begin to dismantle the wall that has been there between Jews and Christians for centuries by melting the mortar of the stone wall… *with our tears.*

Will you pray this repentance prayer with me?

Abba, I confess to You that I still have places in my heart that are stony. I have followed the rituals and traditions of man, and I have not really known You or been obedient to Your holy Word.

Abba, I repent of ever considering the idea that part of Your Word has been overturned and made null and void. I repent of standing apart from parts of Your Word and looking at it as a relic or artifact rather than as a living, breathing expression of Yourself. Abba, I repent and return to following the fullness of Your Word — from Genesis to Revelation.

Abba, I repent of the pride and self righteousness that has been in my own heart in thinking that I am somehow spiritually superior to the Jews. Abba, I give You permission to reveal places in my heart where I still carry arrogance and don't even know it. Abba, would You please do a fresh work in my heart by Your spirit?

> *"A new heart also will I give you, and a new spirit will I put within you: and I will take away the stony heart out of your flesh, and I will give you a heart of flesh. And I will put my spirit within you, and cause you to walk in my statutes, and ye shall keep my judgments, and do them."* EZEKIEL 36:26-27 (KJV)

ENDNOTES:

1.   In 165, Justin and his disciples were arrested for their faith. When the Roman prefect, Rusticus, threatened them with death, Justin said, "If we are punished for the sake of our LORD Jesus Christ, we hope to be saved." They were then taken out and beheaded. Since he gave his life for the faith, Justin was surnamed Martyr, the term now used for those who die for their faith in Christ.

2.   http://www.earlychristianwritings.com/text/justinmartyr-dialoguetrypho.html

Constantine: Following the Road to Rome... or to Jerusalem?

by Laura Densmore

Another Church forefather that we can examine is Constantine (*see entries on The LIST, 315 and 321*).

After the Romans put down the rebellion of 70–71 CE, they destroyed Jerusalem and the Holy Temple. Some Jews ended up in slavery, many died, and others fled for their lives. Jerusalem was renamed Aelia Capitolina and a temple of Zeus was placed on the location of the former Jerusalem Temple.[1] For the next 240 years, early believers were persecuted by the Roman Empire and they scattered and went underground.

The Roman emperor, Constantine, is known for ending the persecution against the early believers of Jesus. In 313 CE, he played a role in the proclamation of the Edict of Milan which:

- declared religious tolerance for Christianity in the Roman Empire and
- made Christianity the new "state" religion.

These are all positives, but to be fair, we need to look at the whole picture.

While the Edict of Milan did extend religious tolerance to Christians in ending persecution against Christians, at the same time this new edict severed the early Church from its Hebrew roots. How is that so? By:

- changing the day of worship from the Sabbath to Sunday, and

- moving away from the biblical feasts and replacing them with Christmas and Easter.

In 325 CE, Constantine called the first Council of Nicea[2] from which we have the Nicene Creed[3] today. This council made many important decisions that still have an enormous influence on the Church to this day. This was a defining moment in the journey of the early Church when our forefathers made a decision to depart from the road to Jerusalem and began going down the road to Rome instead.

At the conclusion of the Nicene Council, Constantine issued a letter to the churches concerning Easter (*emphasis mine*):

> "... At the council we also considered the issue of our holiest day, Easter, and it was determined by common consent that everyone, everywhere should celebrate it on one and the same day... it seemed very unworthy for us to keep this most sacred feast following the custom of the Jews, a people who have soiled their hands in a most terrible outrage, and have thus polluted their souls, and are now deservedly blind. Since we have cast aside their way of calculating the date of the festival, we can ensure that future generations can celebrate this observance at the more accurate time which we have kept from the first day of the passion until the present time. **Therefore have nothing in common with that most hostile people, the Jews. We have received another way from the Savior.**"

Here is an interesting parallel that many have noticed: when the Church fathers departed from following the Hebrew Scriptures (the Old Testament), they also departed from the Jewish people!

And so, wielding the powerful Roman "unholy ax", Constantine began to hack away at and cut off the early Church from observing and keeping the Hebrew scriptures (or Old Testament), and began building the wall of separation between Jews and Christians.

In the year 321 CE, the first Sunday Law was enacted by the Emperor Constantine.[4]

Constantine's decree stated the following:

> "On the venerable Day of the Sun let the magistrates and people residing in cities rest, and let all workshops be closed. In the country, however, persons engaged in agriculture may freely and lawfully continue their pursuits; because it often happens that another day is not so suitable for grain-

sowing or for vine-planting; lest by neglecting the proper moment for such operations the bounty of heaven should be lost."

Constantine's predecessor, Emperor Aurelian, made Sol Invictus an official cult alongside traditional Roman cults. Constantine's new decree was about "sun worship", or the worship of Sol Invictus.[5] "Sun Day" was the day the pagan Romans worshipped the sun.

Though Constantine made Christianity the state religion, there was "mixture" in its practice; the worship of the God of Israel was mixed with worship of the sun, Sol Invictus. Official Roman coinage continued to bear images of Sol, and a gold medallion (pictured right) depicts Constantine's bust twinned with Sol.

A gold coin struck in 313 CE, depicting Constantine as the companion of Sol Invictus, the sun god.

Constantine's triumphal arch was carefully positioned to align with the colossal statue of Sol by the Colosseum, so that Sol formed the dominant backdrop when seen from the direction of the main approach towards the arch.

Constantine's Triumphal Arch, south side, from Via Triumphalis, Coliseum to right.

The purpose of Constantine's decree was to mainstream the practice of "sun worship" and to incorporate that practice into the new state religion of Christianity. In a nutshell, religious practices were being introduced, then later codified and institutionalized — which were a complete departure from the Hebrew Scriptures.

The beginnings of Replacement Theology can be traced to man-made traditions and decrees that began to supersede — and replace — the Hebrew Scriptures. Constantine played a role in formalizing and institutionalizing Replacement Theology. Exactly what is Replacement Theology?

Replacement Theology was first introduced to the Church shortly after gentile leadership took over from Jewish leadership in Jerusalem. The beliefs of Replacement Theology are the following:[6]

1. The Jewish people are now no longer "God's chosen people."

2. In the New Testament, after Pentecost, the term "Israel" refers to the Church.

3. The Mosaic or "Old" covenant (Exodus 20) is now REPLACED by the "New" covenant. Therefore, a great emphasis is placed on New Testament teachings, and Old Testament teachings are de-emphasized.

4. Actual circumcision is replaced by circumcision of the heart.

Here is a question to consider:

When our Church forefathers no longer highly valued, treasured, or followed the Word of God (all of it, from Genesis to Revelation) and, instead, put their focus solely on the New Testament, why did this happen in the same period of time in which they no longer valued and treasured His chosen people, the Jews, who gave us the Hebrew scriptures (the Old Testament)?

Here is another question to also consider:

What would happen if we, in the Church, began to treasure, highly value and follow ALL of the Word of God, (including the Old Testament/ Hebrew scriptures)? And if by so doing, would we also begin to value and treasure His chosen people, the Jews?

I believe that the original decisions by Constantine and the Council of Nicea put the Church forefathers onto a road that led us away from Jerusalem, *and instead put the Church on a road to Rome.* The Church has been on this road for a very long time. Each one of us was "born" into the culture of our time; we have inherited this journey on the road to Rome from our Church forefathers.

Could it be that we have inherited lies from our Church forefathers? If so, how do we go about identifying and replacing those lies with truth?

"O LORD, my strength, and my fortress, and my refuge in the day of affliction, the Gentiles shall come unto thee from the ends of the earth, and

shall say, Surely our fathers have inherited lies, vanity, and things wherein there is no profit." JEREMIAH 16:18 (KJV)

We haven't really taken the time (until now) to question how we got onto this road to Rome, or to ask why we are even on this road? Have we, in the Church, somehow lost our way?

Many are beginning to wake up and turn their hearts back to Jerusalem... and to the Jewish people.

It is in Jerusalem that Yeshua will rule and reign for a thousand years. (Revelation 20:4)

It is in Jerusalem that Yeshua will teach the Torah to all nations. (Isaiah 2:3-4)

It is in Jerusalem that we will meet up with our long lost brothers and sisters, the Jewish people. (Hosea 1:11)

It is in Jerusalem where YHVH places HIS name. (Deuteronomy 16:2, 6, 11)

It is prophesied in the Bible that in the last days, the people of God will ask the way to Zion and to Jerusalem:

> *"In those days, and in that time, says the LORD, the children of Israel shall come, they and the children of Judah together, going and weeping: they shall go, and seek the LORD their God. They shall ask the way to Zion with their faces thitherward, saying, Come, and let us join ourselves to the LORD in a perpetual covenant that shall not be forgotten."* JEREMIAH 50:4-5 (KJV)

Will you pray this repentance prayer with me?

Abba, we have lost our way. We have been on the road to Rome for a very long time and we are not even sure how we got here. We have devalued the Old Testament (Hebrew Scriptures). We have devalued Your chosen people, the Jews. Abba, we repent for this and we ask for Your mercy. Please forgive us.

Abba, would You please get us back onto Your road leading us back to Jerusalem? Would You please send us Your Shepherd, Yeshua to guide us there? And in this journey, as Yeshua gathers us, His lost sheep, may each one of us reconnect to the Hebrew Scriptures.

Would You please help us to find our way to Zion and to Jerusalem? And, would You please help us to reconnect with our long lost family, the Jewish people? May we love them unconditionally, as we return with broken and contrite hearts.

In Yeshua's name,

Amen.

ENDNOTES:

1. https://www.quora.com/Why-did-Romans-expel-Jews-from-Israel

2. https://www.britannica.com/event/Council-of-Nicaea-Christianity-325

3. https://en.wikipedia.org/wiki/Nicene_Creed

4. http://biblelight.net/sunday.htm and https://en.wikipedia.org/wiki/Sunday

5. https://en.wikipedia.org/wiki/Sol_Invictus

6. https://carm.org/questions-replacement-theology

40 days to 9-av 2019

Day 12: July 14, 2019

40 days to Yom Kippur 2019

Day 12: September 11, 2019

Fill in the blank

Day 12: _____

The Nicene Council

by Amy Cogdell

Many Christians recognize the Council of Nicea as a triumph in our history. It was the first worldwide gathering of bishops called to unite the Church around the question of Jesus' divinity. After centuries of debate, our Church forefathers agreed on language describing the mystery of the Son's relation to the Father:

> *"And in one LORD Jesus Christ, the Son of God, begotten of the Father [the only-begotten; that is, of the essence of the Father, God of God, Light of Light, very God of very God, begotten, not made, being of one substance with the Father..."*[1]

Seventeen centuries later, the Nicene Creed remains one of the most universally accepted summaries of Christian doctrine.

Yet for Jewish believers, the Nicene Council must have felt more like a divorce than a victory. Among the Council's proclamations was an order standardizing the date for Easter and separating that date from the Jewish Passover (*see entry on The LIST, 325*). Severing the Christian calendar from the Jewish calendar was the natural fruit resulting from years of polemic against Jews. Gentile leaders of the Church had long portrayed the Jews as a defeated people who had forfeited their claim on the promises of God. Eradicating this lingering link of common ground with Jewish believers must have seemed reasonable and desirable to our Nicene fathers.

However, in doing so I believe they grieved the heart of God. They flattened and skewed the mystery of the Church by untethering it from the mystery of Israel. And they misrepresented the Father's character, for He is a God of unfailing faithfulness and love.

Pictured above: Council of Nicea.

I am writing this reflection as a faithful Catholic. In fact, I am a Protestant who converted to Catholicism. It was the writing of the Nicene and pre-Nicene fathers which drew me. I was captivated by their passion, their depth of insight into scripture, and the paramount importance they placed on unity. Reading their sermons, I felt convicted of my western individualism. I caught a vision for unity rooted in humble submission to Spirit-led authority, and I believed afresh in the wonder of Christ in the Church.

Here are two examples of the writing which moved me so deeply:

> *"When love has entirely cast out fear, and fear has been transformed into love, then the unity brought us by our Savior will be fully realized, for all men will be united with one another through their union with the one supreme God."* St. Gregory of Nyssa (Homily 15: Jaeger VI, 466)

> *"Let us too imitate him (Jesus) and refuse no task, however humble and arduous it may seem, on behalf of those who are our brothers. We may have to serve someone who is small and unimportant if we undertake this work. The job may be very taxing; mountains and precipices may lie in our way; for the sake of our brothers' salvation everything must be endured. God, after all, cares so much for the soul of man that he did not spare even his Son."* St. John Chrysostom (Homily 59)

Recently, I have learned that the men who wrote those homilies also penned these words concerning the Jews (*see entry on The LIST, 335-395*):

> *"Murderers of the LORD, killers of the prophets, enemies and slanderers of God, violators of the law, adversaries of grace, aliens to the faith of their fathers, advocates of the devil, progeny of poison snakes... whose minds are held in darkness, filled with the anger of the Pharisees, a sanhedrin of satans. Criminals, degenerates... enemies of all that is decent and beautiful..."* St. Gregory of Nyssa

And now, listen to the words of John Chrysostom (*see entry on The LIST, 386-87*):

> *"It is because you killed Christ. It is because you stretched out your hand against the LORD. It is because you shed the precious blood that there is now no restoration, no mercy anymore and no defense..."* St. John Chrysostom

How should I respond to this tension as a Catholic? The fathers who crafted the Creed I hold dear, the bishops who spoke so powerfully of unity and compassion, also vilified Jews, incited the faithful to hatred, and sometimes to violence. They stripped the Church of her Jewish witness by suppressing any covenant observance on the part of Jewish believers. They went so far as to contradict the prophets and bind the gospel of grace in claiming there is "no restoration and no mercy" for the Jew. To see such words attributed to saints pains me.

I pray my Church will bring this history to light, mourn over these words, renounce, reject and repudiate them, and ask for pardon.

If Christians had not divorced themselves so thoroughly from the people of Israel, perhaps the Church would better understand her own complex history. We learn in the Old Testament that the calling of God does not prevent a holy people from falling into error. Israel often strayed from God's commands and suffered for her sin. However, God repeatedly sent prophets calling His people to repentance. He never revoked His promises and He never stopped loving Israel.

Both Christians and Jews have been entrusted with holy gifts for blessing the world. Both bear witness to God's Name through their worship and writings. Both have seen God work miracles through men and women of faith. And both, at times, have fallen gravely short in their callings.

There is only one reason the Christian Church exists two thousand years after the death of Jesus. It is the same reason the Jewish people have survived. God loves His people with unending faithfulness. As we Christians contemplate such astounding favor, our hearts should be inflamed with wonder and gratitude. We should love what God loves and desire what He desires. God loves His people and desires to be glorified in them — both Israel and the Church joined to them in the Messiah.

Will you pray this repentance prayer with me?

Father,

I ask You to bring to light the sin of Jewish hatred sown early and deeply into the fabric of Christian thought. I ask you to give us gentile Christians grace to mourn this darkness and the violence it birthed. I ask You, Father, to renew our minds and instruct us in Your faithfulness. I ask You to glorify Yourself in the people of Israel and in the Church, that we may worship You rightly. And I pray the Passover will become a celebration which unites Your people, both Jew and Christian, in joyful hope and thankfulness.

Amen.

ENDNOTES:

1. https://en.wikipedia.org/wiki/Nicene_Creed#Comparison_between_Creed_of_325_and_Creed_of_381

Evil Seeds, Evil Roots and Evil Fruit

by Laura Densmore

We continue the repentance journey of taking an up close and personal look at the sins of our Church forefathers.

One of those Church forefathers was John Chrysostom. He was the Archbishop of Constantinople in the 5th Century, and is considered to be an eminent 'Early Church Father'. He was renowned for his public speaking and preaching. In the Catholic, Anglican and Eastern Orthodox Churches he has been honored as one of the founding Church forefathers and he is referred to as "Saint" John Chrysostom.

Here are a few famous John Chrysostom quotes:[1]

"If you cannot find Christ in the beggar at the church door, you will not find Him in the chalice."

"Prayer is the place of refuge for every worry, a foundation for cheerfulness, a source of constant happiness, a protection against sadness."

"No matter how just your words may be, when you speak with anger, you ruin all: no matter how boldly you speak, how fairly reprove, or whatnot."

"Let us always guard our tongue; not that it should always be silent, but that it should speak at the proper time."

The quotes above sound good and seem to line up with the scriptures; they are the kind of quotes one might put on a refrigerator magnet. But there is a darker side to John Chrysostom that we must look at to understand the complete picture.

In 386-87, John Chrysostom delivered a series of eight hate-filled homilies directed at the Jews, called Adversus Judaeos, "Against the Jews".[2] Here are some of Chrysostom's own words (*see entry on The LIST for Homily VI, 386-387*):

> *"It is because you killed Christ. It is because you stretched out your hand against the* LORD. *It is because you shed the precious blood that there is now no restoration, no mercy anymore and no defense… Through your madness against Christ you have committed the ultimate transgression. This is why you are being punished now worse than in the past. If this were not the case God would not have turned his back on you so completely."*

> *"You did slay Christ, you did lift violent hands against the Master, you did spill his precious blood. This is why you have no chance for atonement, excuse, or defense… Your mad rage against Christ, the Anointed One, left no way for anyone to surpass your sin. This is why the penalty you now pay is greater than that paid by your fathers. If this is not the reason for your present disgrace, why is it that God put up with you in the old days when you sacrificed your children to idols, but turns himself away from you now when you are not so bold as to commit such a crime?… This is why I hate the Jews. Although they possess the Law, they put it to outrageous use."*

Pictured above: John Chrysostom.

In these eight homilies, he says the following:

Regarding the Jews: he likens them to *"dogs"*, *"mad horses"*, *"wolves"*, *"wild beasts"*, *"pigs"*, *"goats"*; he calls them *"the most miserable and wretched of all men"*; and says that *"demons dwell in their souls"*, *"they are fit for killing… while they were making themselves unfit for work, they grew fit for slaughter"*, *"they live for their bellies, they gape for the things of this world, their condition is not better than that of pigs or goats because of their wanton ways and excessive gluttony."*

Regarding the synagogue: *"the synagogue is not only a brothel and a theater; it also is a den of robbers and a lodging for wild beasts"*; and *"Indeed* *the synagogue is less deserving of honor than any inn. It is not merely a lodging place for robbers and cheats but also for demons. This is true not only of the synagogues but also of the souls of the Jews."*

Regarding the Temple: *"The temple was already a den of thieves when the Jewish commonwealth and way of life still prevailed. Now you give it a name more worthy than it deserves if you call it a brothel, a stronghold of sin, a lodging place for demons, a fortress of the devil, the destruction of the soul, the precipice and pit of all perdition, or whatever other name you give it."*

These hate filled words came out of the mouth of John Chrysostom. In stunning irony, the name Chrysostom means "golden-mouthed"!

These words, these "evil seeds of hate" that came out of this "golden-mouthed" man fell into fertile soil. These seeds incubated in the fertile soil of the hearts and minds of the early Church forefathers. These seeds sank their roots deep. Green seedlings sprang upward and grew into thorny bushes with a very deep and expansive root system. An evil fruit sprang forth from these thorny bushes. What was that fruit?

The suggestion to "hate the Jews", to regard them as "wild beasts, pigs, goats", and that they are "fit for slaughter" — these words and ideas became the "idea template" for the Inquisitions, the Crusades and the Holocaust.

You can chop a thorny bush down, but if you don't pull it out by the roots, it will grow right back. The words, the thoughts, and the ideas of Chrysostom can be likened to the roots of the bush.

We can repent of the evil fruit that the bush produced, (the events, the actions and the evil crimes perpetrated against the Jews), but if we don't get to the "roots" of the bush, that evil fruit is bound to spring up again!

What are the "roots" of this? I believe it is a matter of the heart.

How can such hate filled words come from a renowned early Church forefather? What was in this man's heart? The Bible gives us the answer:

"A good man out of the good treasure of his heart brings forth good; and an evil man out of the evil treasure of his heart brings forth evil. For out of the **abundance of the heart his mouth speaks.** *Luke 6:45* (NKJV, emphasis mine)

The mindset and the heart attitude that I heard in my heart as I pondered the words of John Chrysostom was the attitude of spiritual superiority, arrogance and pride. That is the "root" of the matter.

It is for us to repent, not only for the evil fruit, but also of the evil roots… so that this thorny bush with its evil fruit can be chopped down all the way to the roots.

Will you pray this repentance prayer with me?

Father God, I repent of these evil words spoken against the Jewish people by my Church forefather, John Chrysostom. Those evil and hateful words took root in the soil in the hearts and minds of generations of Church believers and produced very evil fruit. Father God, I repent and ask Your forgiveness for the spiritual pride and arrogance of John Chrysostom and our other Church forefathers.

Would You please take out the heart of stone, remove the spiritual pride and arrogance, and the sense of superiority in me? I repent. I ask for Your forgiveness. Take the pride in me out by the ROOT. I apply the blood of Yeshua to my heart, my mind, my thoughts, and my soul. Please change my heart. Change my mind. Change my thoughts.

Father God, would You please give me YOUR HEART for the Jewish people?

Would You please allow me to be a humble servant to my fellow Jewish brothers and sisters? Please give me a deep love for the Jewish people. Please open a door for me to show and demonstrate that love in tangible and practical ways.

In Yeshua's name,

Amen and amen.

ENDNOTES:

1. https://www.azquotes.com/author/21940-Saint_John_Chrysostom

2. https://en.wikisource.org/wiki/Eight_Homilies_Against_the_Jews

Saint (?) Chrysostom: Against the Jews

by Ray Montgomery

"The tongue has the power of life and death, and those who love it will eat its fruit." PROVERBS 18:21 (NIV)

John Chrysostom (c. 349-407) is considered a Doctor of the Church[1], and one of the four Great Greek Fathers (*see entries on The LIST, 386-387*). During his first two years as a presbyter in Antioch (386-387), he denounced Jews and Judaising Christians in *Adversus Judaeos* ("Against the Jews"), a series of eight homilies directed to members of his church who continued to observe Jewish feasts and fasts. Critical of this, he cast Judaism and the synagogues in a negative light. He pictured the Jews as a demon-possessed people who could never be forgiven, concluding that it was the responsibility of Christians to hate Jews. In everything he wrote he used Scripture extensively to "justify" the points he was making!

Here is a sampling from his first Homily (*emphases mine*):[2]

> *"But do not be surprised that I called the Jews pitiable. They really are pitiable and miserable. When so many blessings from heaven came into their hands, they thrust them aside and were at great pains to reject them... Although those Jews had been called to the adoption of sons, they fell to kinship with dogs...*
>
> *But see how thereafter the order was changed about: they became dogs, and we became the children.*

... When brute animals feed from a full manger, they grow plump and become more obstinate and hard to hold in check; they endure neither the yoke, the reins, nor the hand of the charioteer. Just so the Jewish people were driven by their drunkenness and plumpness to the ultimate evil; they kicked about, they failed to accept the yoke of Christ, nor did they pull the plow of his teaching. Another prophet hinted at this when he said: 'Israel is as obstinate as a stubborn heifer' [Hosea 4:16]. And still another called the Jews 'an untamed calf' [Jeremiah 31:18].

Although such beasts are unfit for work, they are fit for killing. *And this is what happened to the Jews: while they were making themselves unfit for work, they grew fit for slaughter... The man who fasts should be properly restrained, contrite, humbled—not drunk with anger... now when [they] fast, they go in for excesses and the ultimate licentiousness, dancing with bare feet in the marketplace... But these Jews are gathering choruses of effeminates and a great rubbish heap of harlots; they drag into the synagogue the whole theater, actors and all. For there is no difference between the theater and the synagogue.*

Many, I know, respect the Jews and think that their present way of life is a venerable one. This is why I hasten to uproot and tear out this deadly opinion. I said that the synagogue is not only a brothel and a theater... it also is a den of robbers and a lodging for wild beasts.

But the Jews... live for their bellies, they gape for the things of this world, their condition is not better than that of pigs or goats because of their wanton ways and excessive gluttony. They know but one thing: to fill their bellies and be drunk...

... Indeed the synagogue is less deserving of honor than any inn. It is not merely a lodging place for robbers and cheats but also for demons. This is true not only of the synagogues but also of the souls of the Jews...

But heaven forbid that I call these people faithful... For, tell me, is not the dwelling place of demons [synagogues] a place of impiety even if no god's statue stands there? Here the slayers of Christ gather together, here the cross is driven out, here God is blasphemed, here the Father is ignored, here the Son is outraged, here the grace of the Spirit is rejected. ***Does not greater harm come from this place since the Jews themselves are demons?***

So the godlessness of the Jews and the pagans is on a par. But the Jews practice a deceit which is more dangerous. In their synagogue stands an invisible altar of deceit on which they sacrifice not sheep and calves but the souls of men.

Certainly it is the time for me to show that demons dwell in the synagogue, not only in the place itself but also in the souls of the Jews…

Do you see that demons dwell in their souls and that these demons are more dangerous than the ones of old? And this is very reasonable. In the old days the Jews acted impiously toward the prophets; now they outrage the Master of the prophets. Tell me this. Do you not shudder to come into the same place with men possessed, who have so many unclean spirits, who have been reared amid slaughter and bloodshed?… Must you not turn away from them since they are the common disgrace and infection of the whole world?… They sacrificed their own sons and daughters to demons… they became more savage than any wild beast.

What else do you wish me to tell you? Shall I tell you of their plundering, their covetousness, their abandonment of the poor, their thefts, their cheating in trade? The whole day long will not be enough to give you an account of these things. But do their festivals have something solemn and great about them? They have shown that these, too, are impure. Listen to the prophets; rather, listen to God and with how strong a statement he turns his back on them: "I have found your festivals hateful, I have thrust them away from myself". [paraphrase of Isaiah 1:13-15]

Do not regard my words lightly. Be scrupulous in hunting out those who suffer from this sickness. Let the women search for the women, the men for the men, the slaves for the slaves, the freemen for the freemen, and the children for the children…"

This sample contains 835 words; the full sermon is 8,600 words, more than ten times longer! And this is only his first Homily; there are seven more along the same lines and with the same thoughts. It is not hard to imagine the effect his powerful words would have had on his congregation, from a man as esteemed as he was, coming from the position of authority he held. Nor is it hard to see why Christians during the Middle Ages began associating Jews with the Devil. And once that association was made…

His influence on church teachings is interwoven throughout the current Catechism of the Catholic Church, and he is cited in 18 sections. He has been referred to as *"one of the most eloquent preachers who ever since apostolic times have brought to men the divine tidings of truth and love"*, and a *"bright, cheerful, gentle soul; a sensitive heart."*[1] He is honoured as a saint with various feast days in different branches of Christendom, and is one of the most prolific authors in the early Church.

But during World War II, his works were frequently quoted and reprinted as a witness for the prosecution by the Nazi Party, in an attempt to legitimize the Holocaust in the eyes of German and Austrian Christians. It is also noteworthy that all neo-Nazi websites today appearing in web searches use his words to support their virulent antisemitic views.

Curiously, Chrysostomos means "golden-mouthed" in Greek, and denotes his celebrated eloquence. But this is a double-edge sword, for *"The tongue has the power of life — and death."* Proverbs 18:21 (NIV). This is why I questioned whether he deserves the title "Saint" in the heading to this devotion.

Will you pray this repentance prayer with me?

Heavenly Father,

We have seen how the tongue can have the power of death, inciting the historical mistreatment of the Jews, and today, still inciting the flames of antisemitism.

But the tongue also has the power of life, and today we use our tongues to repent, and ask for forgiveness for the damage our Church forefathers' words have wreaked. We pray that You would use the power of our words of confession to break the enduring curse they have had throughout history on Your people.

And as we repent we ask that You would fill our mouths with words of healing and comfort. Redeem the words of the past by pouring out Your spirit in these days, raising up legions of men and women who might speak words that overwhelm the destructive "eloquence" of the past with new, life-giving eloquent words that are truly apples of gold in settings of silver. Words that will bless the Jewish people, the nation of Israel, and in so doing will bless the nations of the earth as well.

In Jesus' name,

Amen.

ENDNOTES:

1. https://en.wikipedia.org/wiki/John_Chrysostom
2. https://en.wikisource.org/wiki/Eight_Homilies_Against_the_Jews

Replacement Theology: A Better Question

by Bob O'Dell

Justin Martyr in his fictional work, Dialogue with a Jew, is generally considered to be the first of the Church forefathers to espouse Replacement Theology, when he wrote in about 150 CE:

"As, therefore, Christ is the Israel and the Jacob, even so we, who have been quarried out from the bowels of Christ, are the true Israelitic race." (see entry in The LIST, 155-160)

After Melito of Sardis became the first person on record to say that the Jews killed God, in 167 CE, a number of others would weigh in on various aspects of Replacement Theology, as covered in The LIST:

- Irenaeus in 180 CE
- Tertullian's Apologeticus in 197 CE
- Origen's Declaration in 220 CE
- St. Cyprian in about 249 CE
- Eusebius of Emesa in about 300 CE
- Council of Nicea in 325 CE

The Council of Nicea would begin the process of institutionalizing Replacement Theology in Church practice, first by forcibly separating and renaming the celebration of Christ's resurrection as "Easter" from the Passover week's celebration by the Jews.

Today, Replacement Theology, which is also called supersessionism, is usually defined as the idea that the Church has replaced Israel as the people of God. Very few theologians would self-identify as espousing Replacement Theology. However, the more positive term "Covenant theology" is sometimes used by some, given that all the arguments centering around Replacement Theology find their basis springing from the concept of the New Covenant as mentioned in the New Testament, and Jeremiah 31.

In his book, *Father Forgive Us*, Fred Wright on p. 135[1] identifies four main propositions of Replacement Theology, which are quoted below:

1. *"The modern State of Israel is a theological aberration, a freak of history or simply irrelevant.*

2. *Israel has been replaced by the church in the purposes of God. The scripture, prophecies and promises are now the exclusive property of the church.*

3. *Israel and the Jewish people are now a theological irrelevancy. One stream of thought contends that the Jewish people were used to prepare the way for the Messiah. With the Christ event, this particular period of salvation history came to an end and the church is a new expression of God's election and saving power. Another stream proposes that the church is the continuation of Israel. Israel in this context loses its geographical, ethnic and spiritual identity and the term becomes a generalization for the believing community.*

4. *The extreme right wing of the Replacement Theology group claims that as the Jews rejected Jesus, God has now rejected them. The Jewish people have no destiny, no elective distinction, and no calling. It is not proper to speak of Jews any more. Jews in Israel are Israelis, Jews in America are Americans, and so on. The only way that a Jewish person has any relevance is when he accepts Jesus as personal savior and becomes a member of the Church."*

The worldwide Church would be making a huge, positive step forward if two billion Christians were to each denounce the four points above! Many pro-Israel Christians work to this end, to expose the tenets (listed above) in the Church, and to replace them with the clear teaching across the entire Bible. Indeed, it is very difficult to bend the totality of scriptures in both Old and New Testaments far enough to make an actual case for the beliefs of Replacement Theology. For any scripture that can be bent towards such ideas, I would venture that pro-Israel Christians can offer ten scriptures that both contextualize it, redeem it, and then overwhelm it (that negative sounding verse) with God's goodness and covenant promises towards Israel and the Jewish people.

Replacement Theology is present everywhere because it is taught as axiom in most seminaries! There is no debate in their courses, no alternative view offered to those who would take on the title of Doctor or Reverend and lead large congregations around the world. Therefore those leaders who espouse Replacement Theology rarely identify it as such, nor openly offer the possibility of a different view. It becomes, therefore, a belief that generally "sits within the hearts of those who attend churches", rather than becoming a topic of discussion. Because of this, those who want to "do the work of the Kingdom" by standing against Replacement Theology, must do so by stirring up conversation, and bringing up subjects that others would prefer not to discuss. In other words, they are *troublemakers*!

If you have ever spoken to *even one person* on *even one occasion* against Replacement Theology, then may the LORD bless you! You are my hero!

However, as we begin to turn this devotional towards prayer, I want to speak specifically towards those readers who HAVE spoken out against Replacement Theology on multiple occasions!

I believe that in the process of engaging in this work, we who are believers in Yeshua as the Messiah, who stand against Replacement Theology, have made a mistake of our own: we have, ourselves, fallen into the same trap as Replacement Theology defines, by creating an "us" versus "them" grouping. Whereas Replacement Theology separates and exalts Christians over Jews, we who stand against Replacement Theology, are also falling into a trap of separating ourselves from *fellow Christians* who believe in Replacement Theology and exalting ourselves over them.

I have seen it come out subtly as well! For instance, a pro-Israel Christian may declare proudly, "I stand against Replacement Theology", or may say "I don't believe in Replacement Theology". While neither of these statements is wrong, I believe that declarative statements like that create a category, and we set ourselves up in our hearts to imply an "us" versus "them" scenario. I am part of the better group, the "us", while others are part of that *lesser* group, the "them". That thought carries within it the echo of the very problem of separation and exaltation that we are condemning!

The person I just described is not a "them". I describe myself! This is how I first behaved (at least deep down in my heart), once I was awakened to the false teaching of Replacement Theology. But one day the LORD surprised me, and suggested that perhaps I needed to heed the words of one of the best sermons I had ever heard, whose punchline was that when considering our relationship to those around us, in our neighborhoods and cities: "There is no *them*, only *us*".

In that context, I have decided that there is a better question. I have found that rather than asking:

Do I believe in Replacement Theology?

I should be asking

Is there still any attitude of Replacement still lingering inside me?

In other words, to ask God to *"search me and know my heart and see if there is any wicked way within me"* (Psalm 139:23-24, *my paraphrase*).

I now see that expunging Replacement Theology is not just a room that you can exit instantaneously, but a journey of discovery of what attitudes of Replacement still exist within. I may say a forceful NO to each of the four tenets of Replacement Theology above, but I no longer believe that if I say NO to those four statements, that means that the work within me is done.

At this point, I suppose I could begin telling you about more places in which I have discovered Replacement Theology still within me. But that is not my purpose today. My purpose is to ask if YOU will consider asking God to open up your heart and show you where Replacement Theology might still exist within you. If we all pray that open-ended prayer together, I believe God can get a lot more accomplished in all of us.

We are all on a journey of discovery. We all have room to grow as we receive the truth and light of God.

Ultimately, there is no "them", there is only "us".

Will you pray this repentance prayer with me?

Father in Heaven,

We thank You that You wrote Your plans and purposes for Israel and the Jewish people in Your Word, and that the Word of the LORD endures forever. We thank You that You are a covenant-making, covenant-keeping God.

But, we also acknowledge that Your work within us is not done.

For those who <u>cannot</u> currently say "NO" to all four tenets of Replacement Theology in this article, pray:

Father, I give you permission to show me, in Your timing, what Your Word has to say about the four items previously listed in this devotional. I ask You for revelation, to know Your truth and Your heart in each of those areas. At the same time I pray that I also increase in my understanding and appreciation of that great promise referred to as the New Covenant, offered to us by Christ in his blood. Teach me Your ways.

For those who <u>can</u> say "NO" to all four tenets in this article, pray:

Father, I give You permission to continue the process of teaching me Your plans and purposes for Israel and the Jews. I give You permission to identify additional aspects of "Replacement" of the Jews or of Israel, that exists within my heart. Continue Your work in me regarding the removing of belief systems and thoughts that are not from You.

And for all:

May we learn even more of how to see our brothers and sisters as walking on a journey, rather than standing in "this room" or "that". May we stop separating ourselves and exalting ourselves over anyone.

In Yeshua's name, we pray.

Amen.

ENDNOTES:

1. Fred Wright, Father, Forgive Us: a Christian Response To the Church's Heritage of Jewish Persecution, (United Kingdom, Monarch Books, 2002), 135-136.

Love Your Neighbor?

By Amy Mucklestone

When asked about the greatest commandment in the Torah, Yeshua replied:

> *"You shall love the LORD your God with all your heart, with all your soul, and with all your mind.' This is the first and great commandment. And the second is like it: 'You shall love your neighbor as yourself.' On these two commandments hang all the Law and the Prophets."* MATTHEW 22:37-40 (NKJV)

At the most basic level of our faith, we find the requirement to love our neighbor. Every one of the crimes committed against the Jewish people reflected on The LIST shows a total failure to apply this simple instruction. It is ironic that our antisemitic ancestors were identifying the Jewish people as the hypocritical Pharisees of the gospels while they themselves were the ones so obviously neglecting *"the weightier matters of the law: justice and mercy and faithfulness."* Matthew 23:23 (ESV)

The question arises: "Who is my neighbor?" When the lawyer in Luke 10 asked Yeshua this question, He responded with the story of the good Samaritan. As His followers, we have the responsibility to "...do good to all people, but especially to those who are of the household of faith." Galatians 6:10 (NASB). We are commissioned to heal the brokenhearted and bind up their wounds — both in the spiritual and the natural:

> *"The Lord does build up Jerusalem: he gathers together the outcasts of Israel. He heals the broken in heart, and binds up their wounds."* PSALM 147:2-3 (KJV 2000)

At HaYovel, we are privileged to work in Israel's vineyards and olive groves, healing the spiritual wounds of the Jewish people by means of natural wine and oil. However, along with the privilege comes the humility of remembering why we are here. We are carrying the burdens of generational blindness, willful ignorance and other unrighteous fruits of Replacement Theology. Nothing we can do can possibly make up for the gross mistreatment, torture and loss of life inflicted by this grave error and recounted so painfully on The LIST.

Reading through the section on Godfrey de Bouillon (*see entry on The LIST, 1099*), I saw my own genealogy reflected. A few years ago, I had some time to look into my ancestry and was surprised to find a Crusader King of Jerusalem in my own family history and lineage (it may or may not have been Godfrey himself). At first I was impressed.

With further reflection, my pride gave way to a deep shame: here was proof that I would not be here, if not for the bloodline of someone so deeply involved in Replacement Theology that he actually presumed to sit on the throne of Jerusalem!

Pictured above: Crusaders in Jerusalem, 1099.

It really struck me that I have a responsibility to do all I can to combat this mindset, even as far downstream as I am, in order to love my neighbor and work against the damage inflicted so long ago by my own forefathers.

"Then the righteous will answer Him, saying, 'LORD, when did we see You hungry and feed You, or thirsty and give You drink? When did we see You a stranger and take You in, or naked and clothe You? Or when did we see You sick, or in prison, and come to You?' And the King will answer and say to them, 'Assuredly, I say to you, inasmuch as you did it to one of the least of these My brethren, you did it to Me. '" MATTHEW 25:37-40 (NKJV, emphasis mine)

This passage clearly indicates that we who claim to follow Yeshua will one day be judged based on our treatment of His family. I tremble to think of that great and terrible day, when those who have perpetrated or agreed with the crimes on The LIST are faced with the consequences of their action—or inaction.

Leviticus 19:16b states:

"...Do not stand idly by while your neighbor's life is threatened. I am the LORD." (NLT)

So many of these atrocities could have been avoided if those who disagreed with the perpetrators had taken the scriptures seriously and stood up to defend His people.

Among all the criminal acts on The LIST, though, I do see a thread of hope. I am so grateful to see included the points at which individuals did stand up to be counted. Right around the time Godfrey was massacring Jews in Jerusalem, the bishop at Cologne, Germany was offering protection for those under his jurisdiction (*see entry on The LIST, 1096*). He later escorted the Jews to towns under his protection.

Frederick Barbarossa, King James I of Aragon, and Pope Gregory X were others in that time period who made strides toward improving things, though sporadically. We can see from these men that individuals do not have to be tied to the sins of their predecessors. We have a choice of whether to participate in those sins or to cut off that heritage and move forward to make restitution. This is part of the great restoration of all things that the prophets foretold.

It is for us now to come in humility from the ends of the Earth and say:

"Surely our fathers have inherited lies, worthlessness and unprofitable things." JEREMIAH 16:19 (NKJV)

May we all aspire to be counted as "righteous among the nations," and be prepared to stand up when the opportunity arises.

Will you pray this repentance prayer with me?

Father God, please forgive me for the sins of my ancestors, and cancel any curses brought on me and on my children by their actions.

Please allow me to serve You in humility and righteousness, and to walk in wisdom according to Your heart and Your ways. Thank You for remaining faithful to Your covenants with the Jewish people and the land of Israel, so that we who are invited to join from the outside have hope that You will not abandon us.

Please give us opportunity to go through the gates, prepare the way for the people, build up the highway, and take out the stones — the stumbling blocks — left behind on Your path.

Please continue to remove the scales from our eyes and turn our stony hearts to flesh.

Thank You for the work You are doing, Abba!

Amen.

Simon of Trent and Host Desecration:
Blood-guiltiness, Which Has Been Forgotten

by Sister Joela

At the end of the 15th Century, the Jewish community of Trent in Northern Italy suddenly found themselves a target of persecution and displacement. But why?

It began centuries earlier at the fourth Synod of the Lateran, when the Roman Catholic view of the Holy Communion became defined (*see entry on The LIST, 1215*):

> "The fourth Lateran Council, also called the Great Council, is where the Catholic doctrine on transubstantiation (where the bread and wine become the actual blood and body of Christ) was defined. Constantine's Sword[1] calls this the most important Council because it systematised anti-Jewish practices at the same time that the Church achieved universal authority, instituting the yellow 'badge of shame' for the Jews..."

This doctrine of "transubstantiation" set the stage for the first case of "host desecration"[2] in Berlitz, near Berlin, just 28 years later (*see entry on The LIST, 1243*).

Host Desecration

According to the doctrine of transubstantiation, a consecrated host wafer becomes the flesh of Jesus Christ. Medieval Christians believed that Jews would steal these consecrated host wafers and desecrate them by stabbing them to make them bleed in order to reenact the crucifixion of Christ. In the 19th Century it was shown that the red color often found on the wafers was due to a fungus.[3]

Jews were also accused of ritually murdering Christian children and using their blood for Jewish religious rituals. Even when the Pope repudiated those stories, it could not erase them from public awareness.

Simon of Trent

So what exactly happened in Trent? In 1475, a 3-year old child named Simon drowned in the river Adige (*see entry on The LIST, 1475*). At the time he just went "missing". On Easter Sunday a Jewish landlord found the child's body on his grounds by the riverbanks. Afraid of slander and misinterpretation, he immediately hurried to the local Bishop to tell about his finding. But Bernardino da Feltre, a fanatical Franciscan monk, immediately put the blame on the Jews. He charged the Jews with using Simon's body for its blood. Seventeen Jews were tortured for two weeks, six Jews were burned and two were strangled. Five years later, a trial was reopened on this matter and five more Jews were executed.

Fresco depicting martyred Simon of Trent.

A process of Inquisition began. As a result of this one incident, the accidental drowning death of a 3-year old boy in 1475, all the Jewish population was expelled from Trent in 1486 for a period of 300 years. Miracles, allegedly released by the mortal remains of Simon, were preached from the pulpits; people started pilgrimages; finally Simon was beatified (the first step toward canonisation)! The printing press had just been invented, so the stories about Simon were widely published. This was, in fact, one of the first media frenzies in history, with this trial being the basis of antisemitic writings for hundreds of years.

In Goethe's lifetime (1749-1832), you could still see a Fresco depicting scenes of the story in the tower of the Old Bridge in Frankfurt. It displays a summary of the most heinous slander against Jews in one painting: beneath the "martyred child" you see a "Jew Pig" in the midst of a group of Jews — and also Satan.

And then rhymes arose, saying:

> *"As known as Trent and the child will have been, the rascal Jew will be clearly seen."*

In 1965 the Catholic Church reinvestigated the story, and declared it to be a fraud. Simon's feast day was removed from the calendar, and his future veneration was officially forbidden.

Host Desecration in 1399

But 76 years before the Simon of Trent incident, Jews in Poznań, Poland, were charged with host wafer desecration, where they were accused of bribing a Christian woman to steal host wafers from a local church (*see entry on The LIST, 1399*). Allegedly, the host wafers were stabbed, then they were bled out and thrown into a well. The Archbishop learned of the "blasphemy" and ordered that the Rabbi, 13 elders and the woman be tied to pillars and roasted alive over a slow fire.

Today "miracle water" that comes from that well is sold at the church, allegedly made "miraculous" because of the host wafers that the Jews tossed into it.

A sign above the faucet loosely translates like a nursery rhyme:

"MIRACULOUS WATER

From the well in which Your Body was drowned

Many sick folks their health have found

But most of all we ask you, LORD

For health of soul to be restored."

Jews stabbing the host wafers with knives. Medieval painting of host desecration by Jews from Museo Nacional d'Art de Catalunya.

Host desecration accusations against the Jews continued for many centuries, with the last recorded accusation occurring in Berlad, Romania, in 1836.[2]

Blood-guiltiness

When the world falls in sin, and we lie, kill, and fight wars, we should not be surprised: our sinful nature is the nature of the "prince of this world". But when the Church starts to lie, kill and fight wars, while she pretends to be "just", she has taken leadership of sin. She has allied herself to Satan - deeper than the world — with the one whom Jesus called the "father of lies" and a "murderer from the beginning" (John 8:44, NIV).

For centuries the enemy was granted rights and claims we still struggle to wrest away from him. The sins of the Church have a deeper and much more devastating impact on the seen and the unseen world.

What a deep grief for God's heart, having sacrificed His only beloved Son for our sake, watching us persecuting, fighting and murdering in the very name of this crucified One. What a grief that we made the most precious gift on earth, His sacrificed body and His shed Jewish blood, a weapon turned against His own people!

Pogroms that were caused by denunciation for ritual murders and for hosts being defiled not only stand against His commandment: *"You shall not bear false witness against your neighbor"* (Exodus 20:16, ESV), but they have also put an enormous bloodguiltiness upon the Church.

We all know about the Holocaust — but what do we know about this guilt?

We are in grave danger to use the same arguments the spiritual leaders used in the time of Jesus:

> *"Woe unto you, scribes and Pharisees, hypocrites! because ye build the tombs of the prophets, and garnish the sepulchres of the righteous, And say, If we had been in the days of our fathers, we would not have been partakers with them in the blood of the prophets... That upon you may come all the righteous blood shed upon the earth, from the blood of righteous Abel unto the blood of Zacharias son of Barachias, whom ye slew between the Temple and the altar."* MATTHEW 23:29-30, 35 (KJV, emphasis mine)

We have considered these verses before the LORD over a number of years, and have reached a vexing conclusion. Unless we repent, the LORD will claim every single person's blood from us, the worldwide Church, which was innocently shed, as long as we continue to consider ourselves superior to our Church forefathers and elevate ourselves above their guilt.

Will you pray this repentance prayer with me?

O LORD, this innocently shed blood cries out to the Heavens — and so few even know about it; and if they knew, they would often shut their eyes. We confess that our attitude against every hard and difficult burden we face is a strong rejection; each time we just want to ignore these facts, which are so terrifying, so depressing, so burdensome. They stir up our ego-centered life. We beg Your forgiveness, and we also pray that Your Love will break through our hard and indifferent hearts.

Please forgive us, we who so cruelly and perversely disfigured Your nature, even while we longed to know You and to love YOU. Forgive us, for our churches and communities which did not walk or show that pathway to repentance. We should know that path better than anyone, and You made it so us easy for us to walk. Heal the deep wounds we have scarred into generations of Your people.

We pray for the many places which became famous by a pack of lies. Their sad past does not touch our conscience as we consider it "cultural history". Would You please bring to light what is in darkness and reveal Yourself as the King of truth and justice? Please change our hearts and set us free into the beauty of Your kindness, humility and mercy.

Amen.

ENDNOTES:

1.   James Carroll, Constantine's Sword: The Church and the Jews, (New York, Houghton Mifflin Harcourt, 2001), 282-83

2.   https://en.wikipedia.org/wiki/Host_desecration

3.   https://www.huffingtonpost.com/2013/06/03/illuminating-faith-eucharist-in-medieval-life-and-art-photos_n_3210234.html

Martin Luther: Spiritual Blindness

by Ray Montgomery

" I f I had been a Jew and had seen such dolts and blockheads govern and teach the Christian faith, I would sooner have become a hog than a Christian. They have dealt with the Jews as if they were dogs rather than human beings; they have done little else than deride them and seize their property. When they baptize them they show them nothing of Christian doctrine or life, but only subject them to popishness and mockery... If the apostles, who also were Jews, had dealt with us Gentiles as we Gentiles deal with the Jews, there would never have been a Christian among the Gentiles... When we are inclined to boast of our position [as Christians] we should remember that we are but Gentiles, while the Jews are of the lineage of Christ. We are aliens and in-laws; they are blood relatives, cousins, and brothers of our LORD. Therefore, if one is to boast of flesh and blood the Jews are actually nearer to Christ than we are... If we really want to help them, we must be guided in our dealings with them not by papal law but by the law of Christian love. We must receive them cordially, and permit them to trade and work with us, that they may have occasion and opportunity to associate with us, hear our Christian teaching, and witness our Christian life. If some of them should prove stiff-necked, what of it? After all, we ourselves are not all good Christians either."

— Martin Luther, **favourable words on Jews in his essay** "That Jesus Christ Was Born a Jew", (*see entry on The LIST, 1523*)

"There is no other explanation for this than the one cited earlier from Moses — namely, that God has struck [the Jews] with 'madness and blindness and confusion of mind' [Deuteronomy 28:28]. So we are even at fault in not avenging all this

*innocent blood of our L*ORD *and of the Christians which they shed for three hundred years after the destruction of Jerusalem, and the blood of the children they have shed since then (which still shines forth from their eyes and their skin).* **We are at fault in not slaying them.**" *(emphasis mine)*

> — Martin Luther, **antisemitic words on Jews** in his essay "On the Jews and Their Lies" (*see entry on The LIST, 1543*)

With the death of the apostles around 100 CE, much of the light in the early Church gradually flickered out, and by the 4th Century, the combination of heresy, compromise and corruption produced a period of spiritual and intellectual darkness and barbarity, known as the Dark Ages, that was to last a thousand years. It was this darkness and corruption that Martin Luther railed against, when he nailed his 95 Theses to the church door at Wittenberg[1], which included the following provocative challenges to the Church (*see entry on The LIST, 1517*):

Pictured above: Martin Luther.

26. The pope does very well when he grants remission to souls in purgatory, not by the power of the keys, which he does not have, but by way of intercession for them.

27. They preach only human doctrines who say that as soon as the money clinks into the money chest, the soul flies out of purgatory.

32. Those who believe that they can be certain of their salvation because they have indulgence letters will be eternally damned, together with their teachers.

36. Any truly repentant Christian has a right to full remission of penalty and guilt, even without indulgence letters.

45. Christians are to be taught that he who sees a needy man and passes him by, yet gives his money for indulgences, does not buy papal indulgences but God's wrath.

49. Christians are to be taught that papal indulgences are useful only if they do not put their trust in them, but very harmful if they lose their fear of God because of them.

But while he launched a much-needed Reformation in the Church (for which he is rightly remembered), how did he transform from being pro-Jewish at the beginning of his career, to being virulently antisemitic a mere 20 years later? Furthermore, why has this fact been largely swept under the rug within Christendom at large?

History shows us that he longed for a unified Protestant society, where Church and state combined to create a community that banished all threatening groups, a sort of Protestant medievalism, if you will.[2] So in response to the Peasants' War in 1524-25, a widespread popular economic and religious revolt against the ruling aristocracy in the German speaking areas around Germany (Alsace, Switzerland and Austria), Luther supported the authorities, even as he sympathised with some of the peasants' grievances, saying in his essay *"Against the Murderous, Thieving Hordes of Peasants"*:[3]

> *"Therefore let everyone who can, smite, slay, and stab, secretly or openly, remembering that nothing can be more poisonous, hurtful, or devilish than a rebel... Our peasants, however, want to make the goods of other men common, and keep their own for themselves. Fine Christians they are! I think there is not a devil left in hell; they have all gone into the peasants. Their raving has gone beyond all measure."*

This reaction alludes to his concern that he might be seen to be responsible for their rebellion. And when the Anabaptists threatened Protestant unity, a memorandum written in 1531 by Luther's colleague Philip Melanchthon[2] (and signed by Luther), argues that such offences merited the death penalty:

> *"Although it seems cruel to punish them with the sword, it is crueler that they condemn the ministry of the Word and have no well-grounded doctrine and suppress the true and in this way seek to subvert the civil order."*

Consequently, Anabaptists were fined, burned at the stake, tortured and persecuted for their beliefs. Thousands were put to death. And because they believed in baptism by full immersion, many were drowned!

But there is a spiritual aspect to this that also needs to be considered, which contains the seeds of deception. This deception caused a spiritual blindness to come upon Luther, making him blind to what the LORD was doing in Christendom. This deception, I believe, led to his later antisemitism.

Beginning with the Reformation, the LORD was restoring truth to His Body, truth that had been lost through corruption, greed and heresy. Luther had discovered this first truth of "justification by faith" (Habakkuk 2:4; Romans 1:17), a truth that shook the religious world in his day to the core, launched a much-needed Reformation (*see entry on The LIST, 1517*), and established the Lutheran denomination in the process.

But in 1525, the Anabaptists (meaning "one who baptises again") restored the truth of water baptism by *full immersion*, which is only possible when the candidate confesses his or her faith in Christ, and wants to be baptised. This belief ran contrary to the baptism of infants as practised by the Church, thus rendering their baptisms null and void. Luther failed to see that this was yet more truth being restored to the Body of Christ, and he resisted it. In effect, he rejected truth, and with his support for the death penalty for those who held such views, this opened him up to spiritual blindness:

> *"Anyone who claims to be in the light but hates a brother or sister is still in the darkness. Anyone who loves their brother and sister lives in the light, and there is nothing in them to make them stumble. But anyone who hates a brother or sister is in the darkness and walks around in the darkness. They do not know where they are going, because the darkness has blinded them."*
> 1 JOHN 2:9-11 (NIV)

Luther not only hated the Jews, but also fellow Christians (Anabaptists; Roman Catholics), and Sabbatarians — both Jews and Christians — who observed the Sabbath on Saturday (*see entry on The LIST for his treatise "Against the Sabbatarians", 1538*). It was this hatred which led to his spiritual blindness, resulting from the rejection of revealed truth, which led him down the path to his later antisemitism.

Luther's legacy is two-fold. He is rightly lauded for restoring the truth of justification by faith, launching the Reformation, and translating the Bible into the language of the common people. But we must also remember his later antisemitism, and the terrible legacy that he left for later generations, for this legacy culminated in Nazi Germany's Holocaust. We must learn the lessons of his spiritual blindness.

"He who has ears to hear, let him hear." MATTHEW 11:15 (ESV)

Will you pray this repentance prayer with me?

Heavenly Father,

We thank You for Martin Luther, for his courage in making a stand for truth, and for exposing the hypocrisy and heresy in the Church. We thank You for the role he played in establishing the Reformation.

But we also ask for forgiveness for his antisemitism, and for the role he played in the terrible legacy that followed, which culminated in the Holocaust. May we learn the lesson he failed to see: that his rejection of truth resulted in spiritual blindness.

As David encouraged us to pray in Psalm 51, we ask You to search our own hearts, to see if there is any aspect of sin You once wished to deal with, but which we hardened our hearts to, and rejected. All You require is obedience, so we ask for Your grace and mercy, to speak to us again, and open our eyes to "the truth, the whole truth, and nothing but the truth". Give us "ears to hear", so that we can repent of our disobedience, and You can restore us.

We ask these things in Your Name,

Amen.

ENDNOTES:

1.   https://www.luther.de/en/95thesen.html

2.   https://www.thegospelcoalition.org/article/luthers-jewish-problem/

3.   http://zimmer.csufresno.edu/~mariterel/against_the_robbing_and_murderin.htm

Sowing and Reaping

by Ray Montgomery

"Hence today I believe that I am acting in accordance with the will of the Almighty Creator: by defending myself against the Jew, I am fighting for the work of the LORD." ~Adolf Hitler[1]

"They will put you out of the synagogue; in fact, the time is coming when anyone who kills you will think they are offering a service to God."
JOHN 16:2 (NIV)

The path to the Holocaust began barely 100 years after the deaths of the apostles. We don't know if the Nazis researched Church canonical law to specifically look for laws they could enact, but their anti-Jewish legislation clearly has precedent in our own antisemitic Church history and theology.

Canonical Law is a body of codified ecclesiastical law, especially of the Roman Catholic Church, as promulgated in ecclesiastical councils and by the pope. The first such council dates back to the Council of Jerusalem (*see entry on The LIST, 50*).

This council set the precedent for future Church councils and synods throughout our Church history. But while the divergent opinions between Judaism and the new gentile Christian perspectives were already evident, this Council was able to resolve their differences amicably. Future Church councils however, would not be so kind or forgiving to the Jews.

The following chart of Canonical Law, resulting from Church councils, is compared to Nazi Measures, and illustrates where the seeds of the Nazi laws originated: they came from our own Church Canonical Laws!

CANONICAL LAW	NAZI MEASURE
Prohibition of intermarriage and of sexual intercourse between Christians and Jews, Synod of Elvira, 306.	Law for the Protection of German Blood and Honor, September 15, 1935 (RGB1 I, 1146).
Jews and Christians not permitted to eat together, Synod of Elvira, 306.	Jews barred from dining cars (Transport Minister to Interior Minister, December 30, 1939, Document NG-3995).
Jews not permitted to show themselves in the streets during Passion Week, 3d Synod of Orleans, 538.	Decree authorizing local authorities to bar Jews from the streets on certain days (i.e., Nazi holidays), December 3, 1933 (RGB1 I, 1676).
Burning of the Talmud and other books, 12th Synod of Toledo, 681.	Book burnings in Nazi Germany.
Construction of new synagogues prohibited, Council of Oxford, 1222.	Destruction of synagogues in entire Reich, November 10, 1938 (Heydrich to Göring, November 11, 1938, PS-3058).
Christians not permitted to sell or rent real estate to Jews, Synod of Ofen, 1279.	Decree providing for compulsory sale of Jewish real estate, December 3, 1938 (RGB1 I, 1709).
Jews not permitted to obtain academic degrees, Council of Basel, 1434, Sessio XIX.	Law against Overcrowding of German Schools and Universities, April 25, 1933 (RGB1 I, 225).

Partially quoted from the book "Christian Antisemitism: A History of Hate" by William Nichols[2]

Nazi book burnings.

Sowing and Reaping

The Bible says:

> *Do not be deceived: God cannot be mocked. A man reaps what he sows.*
> GALATIANS 6:7 (NIV)

A 19th Century aphorism powerfully states:

> *Sow a thought, reap an action;*
>
> *Sow an action, reap a habit;*
>
> *Sow a habit, reap a character;*
>
> *Sow a character, reap a destiny.*

Now, with The LIST in one hand and this aphorism in the other, it is possible to see how it played out in history.

"Sow a thought, reap an action"

Sowing: The following "thoughts" were sown by our Church forefathers (*see entries on The LIST for the respective years for all quotes and Papal bulls*):

> *"The LORD is insulted, God has been murdered, the King of Israel has been destroyed by the right hand of Israel."* Melito of Sardis, bishop, early Church authority, c. 167 CE

> *"The Jews have rejected the Son of God and cast Him out of the vineyard when they slew Him. Therefore, God has justly rejected them and has given to the Gentiles outside the vineyard the fruits of its cultivation."* Irenaeus, Greek cleric who developed Christian theology, c. 180 CE

> *"Scattered in all directions, straggling, exiles from their own soil and sky, they [the Jews] wander over the world without either man or God for their king..."* Tertullian, prolific Christian author, 197 CE

> *"Jews, according to what had before been foretold, had departed from God, and had lost God's favour... while the Christians had succeeded to their place."* St. Cyprian, bishop, c. 246-258

Reaping: antisemitism and Replacement Theology becomes enshrined in Church Canonical Law (see chart above). The persecutions begin.

"Sow an action, reap a habit"

Sowing: Once the first antisemitic Church Laws were passed, the precedent was set, and more followed.

Reaping: With antisemitism and Replacement Theology now enshrined in Church Canonical Law, it created an atmosphere where antisemitic writings became the norm:

> *"Indeed the synagogue is less deserving of honor than any inn. It is not merely a lodging place for robbers and cheats but also for demons. This is true not only of the synagogues but also of the souls of the Jews."* St. John Chrysostom, Archbishop of Constantinople, Church father, from Homily I, the first of his eight sermons Against the Jews, 386-87 CE

> *"LET no one in the priestly order nor any layman eat the unleavened bread of the Jews, nor have any familiar intercourse with them, nor summon them in illness, nor receive medicine from them, nor bathe with them…"* Trullo Ecumenical Council, 692 CE

> *"We exhort your Royal Majesty not to further tolerate that the Jews rule Christians and have power over them. For to allow, that Christians are subordinated to Jews and are delivered to their whims, means to oppress the Church of God, means to revile Christ himself."* Pope Gregory VII, 1081 CE

And more persecutions, blood libel accusations, host desecration accusations, murders, and expulsions.

"Sow a habit, reap a character"

Sowing: Antisemitic writings over the centuries became habitual.

Reaping: Papal bulls (edicts issued by a Pope) were issued against the Jews, such as by:

- Pope Innocent III, 1205 CE: accused Jews of usury, blasphemy, arrogance, employing Christian slaves, and murder.
- Pope Boniface VIII, 1299 CE: declared that Jews be included among persons who might be denounced to the Inquisition without the name of the accuser revealed.
- Pope Eugene IV, 1442 CE: required complete separation of Jews and Christians (ghetto).

And more persecutions, blood libel accusations, host desecration accusations, murders, expulsions, ghettos, pogroms, Crusades, Auto-da-fés, and Inquisitions.

"Sow a character, reap a destiny"

Sowing: The Church's antisemitic character now set the stage for Martin Luther's writings, such as On the Jews and Their Lies (*see entry on The LIST, 1543*). He used violent (and vulgar) language to denounce the Jews, and in response to the question: *"What shall we Christians do with this rejected and condemned people, the Jews?"*, he wrote:[3,4,5]

> "First, to set fire to their synagogues or schools…
>
> Second, I advise that their houses also be razed and destroyed…
>
> Third, I advise that all their prayer books and Talmudic writings, in which such idolatry, lies, cursing, and blasphemy are taught, be taken from them…
>
> Fourth…

He concludes his list of "recommendations" with:

> *"…God has struck [the Jews] with 'madness and blindness and confusion of mind' [Deuteronomy 28:28]. So we are even at fault in not avenging all this innocent blood…* **We are at fault in not slaying them.***"* (emphasis mine)

Reaping: Luther would get his wish: the Holocaust!

Himmler, prime architect of the Holocaust, admired Martin Luther's writings, which Karl Jaspers, philosopher, summarized as: "There you have the whole Nazi program."[4]

> ***What a hideous destiny the Jews have reaped***
> ***from the thoughts our original Church forefathers sowed!***

Conclusion

Once our history is laid out bare before us like this, it is hard not to connect the dots and be moved spiritually and emotionally. The evidence is irrefutable. Our guilt is undeniable. The conclusions are inescapable: the law of sowing and reaping meant that the Jews suffered the consequences!

Oh LORD, what have we done…

Will you pray this repentance prayer with me?

Heavenly Father,

With broken hearts we come to You, our bloody history laid bare. We ask for forgiveness for the sins of our Church forefathers who persecuted our Jewish brethren. We acknowledge that these attitudes begin in the heart, and we lay our own hearts bare before You. Search us LORD, to see if we harbour any seeds which may one day yield bitter fruit. May we learn the lesson of sowing and reaping from our repugnant Christian history — of what NOT to sow. Instead, let us only sow "seeds of righteousness" (Hosea 10:12).

In Jesus' name,

Amen.

ENDNOTES:

1. https://en.wikiquote.org/wiki/Religious_views_of_Adolf_Hitler

2. Original research for this chart came from the book The Destruction of the European Jews, by Raul Hilberg, 1961. Thanks also to William Nichols, Christian Antisemitism: A History of Hate, (USA, Rowman & Littlefield, 2004), 204-206; and Baruch Hashem Messianic Synagogue in Dallas, TX for raising awareness of Hillberg's research, and from whom this chart was reproduced.

3. https://en.wikipedia.org/wiki/On_the_Jews_and_Their_Lies

4. https://archive.org/stream/TheJewsAndTheirLies1543En1948/LUTHERDr._Martin-The_Jews_and_their_Lies_1948-EN_djvu.txt (full text)

5. https://en.wikipedia.org/wiki/Martin_Luther_and_antisemitism

Heal My Blind Eyes O Lord! Reflections on Judensau

by Laura Densmore

"For with what judgment you judge, you will be judged; and with the measure you use, it will be measured back to you. And why do you look at the speck in your brother's eye, but do not consider the plank in your own eye? Or how can you say to your brother, 'Let me remove the speck from your eye'; and look, a plank is in your own eye? Hypocrite! First remove the plank from your own eye, and then you will see clearly to remove the speck from your brother's eye." MATTHEW 7:2-5 (NKJV)

If we consider this parable at a deeper level, one could say that it is we Christians who have been trying to remove the speck from our Jewish brothers' eyes: they do not believe that Yeshua is the Messiah. However, we Christians have had planks in our own eyes: we have considered that the Old Testament/Covenant has been overturned and is null and void and it has been "replaced" with the New Testament/Covenant.

Our Church forefathers took up the position that somehow, God was "finished" with the Jews, that the promises and covenants He made to them were only "temporary" and not eternal, and that somehow, God had made a "mistake" in those promises. The conclusion: He replaced his chosen people, the Jews, with the Christian Church. Does God make mistakes? Does He make a promise that is forever eternal and then change His mind to make that be a promise that is only temporary? This does not line up with the nature and character of the God of Israel, nor does it line up with His Word:

> *"Thus says the Lord, which gives the sun for a light by day, and the ordinances of the moon and of the stars for a light by night, which divides the sea when the waves thereof roar; The Lord of hosts is his name: If those ordinances depart from before me, says the Lord, then the seed of Israel also shall cease from being a nation before me forever. Thus says the Lord; If heaven above can be measured, and the foundations of the earth searched out beneath, I will also cast off all the seed of Israel for all that they have done, says the Lord."* JEREMIAH 31:35-37 (KJV)

Can the heavens above be measured? No! Can the foundations of the Earth be searched out? No! Will God ever cast off the seed of Israel? NEVER!

Do we believe in the power of God to fulfill the promises He made to Israel? Do we believe in the unfettered power of God to finish the process He started when He brought His people out of Egypt? For many in the Church today, the answer is no, or there is waffling and wavering doubt. I believe these sins of unbelief and doubt in the Church today need to be exposed and repented of.

This blindness and unbelief is rooted in the sin of pride and self-righteousness. If we've been in church for very many years, we can develop the following mindset:

> *"Well, I'm all right. I don't need to repent of any sin. I go to church every Sunday, (or Sabbath as the case may be), I put my tithe in the offering plate, I don't steal, I don't do drugs, I'm not cheating on my wife/husband, etc. I try to be a good person, so I don't need to repent."*

That is pride. It can be very subtle. It likes to be cloaked and hidden. It is the sin of pride that keeps us blind. So we must begin by repenting of pride. Then we can get to the rest of the hidden sins behind the wall of pride.

As I read through The LIST, there were two items that grabbed my attention:

- Earliest Judensau ("Jew-Pig"; *see entry on The LIST, 1230*). The Judensau erected in the Cathedral of Brandenburg in 1230, Brandenberg, Germany, is the earliest extant example of a Jew-Pig sculpture on a church building.

- Judensau erected in Wittenberg, Germany (*see entry on The LIST, 1305*). While it was erected on a Catholic church in 1305, this same church would become the home church of Martin Luther after he founded the Protestant Reformation in 1517.

What is a "Judensau" I wondered? Not knowing what a Judensau was, I googled it, and was shocked to see images of stone carved pigs on church buildings! I could not believe my eyes.

Pictured above: Stone Judensau affixed to Martin Luther's church in Wittenberg.

Tears flowed. I never knew that "Judensau" figures carved in stone even existed, and that they are attached to churches all over Europe—still to this day! I was blind to their existence. Deep shame and sorrow hit my heart as I gazed upon these images.

In fact, the church where Martin Luther worshipped in Wittenberg has one attached to the outer walls of the church building. On the 500-year anniversary of the birth of the "Protestant Reformation" a petition was put forth to remove the Judensau stone figure from the church.[1] Sadly, the petition was denied (*see entry on The LIST, 2016*). The antisemitic carved figure of the pig was left intact on the church building. Shame on us. Sister Joela, who was involved in bringing this petition forward, tells us more about it in her devotion, "Jew Sow in Wittenberg".

The blindness that we have in the Church has been there for a long time, spanning the centuries. We must take responsibility for the sins of our Church forefathers. We must "own" these sins and our unbelief in the power of God to finish what He started. And then, as the Spirit so moves, we can allow our hearts to be broken because of those sins and iniquities.

"And Jesus said, For judgment I am come into this world, that they which see not might see; and that they which see might be made blind. And some of the Pharisees which were with him heard these words, and said unto him, Are we blind also? Jesus said unto them, If ye were blind, ye should have no sin: but now you say, We see; therefore your sin remains." JOHN 9:39-41 (KJV)

Will you pray this repentance prayer with me?

Abba Father, thank You for revealing to me the "sins of my Church fathers" that is documented in The LIST. I repent of the sin of pride of my Church forefathers.

Father, I confess to You and repent of my own spiritual pride that has kept me blind. I must acknowledge that I am blind also so that You can allow me to see. Father, please heal my blind eyes. Please take the scales off my eyes. Please allow me to "see" the sins of my Church forefathers that I have been blind to.

Would You please use The LIST like a "jackhammer" to break up the cement-like places found in my own heart? Would You please use The LIST as an instrument to bring about deep, heartfelt repentance in me?

May I weep over the things that cause You to weep, and may it be Your tears that slide down my cheeks. May the repentance in me result in deep changes in how I think, how I believe, and how I behave towards the Jewish people.

In Yeshua's name,

Amen and amen!

Endnotes:

1. https://www.thelocal.de/20171031/anti-jewish-sculpture-splits-opinion-on-500-anniversary-reformation-wittenber-luther

How Do We Buy Salve for Our Blind Eyes O Lord?

by Donna Jollay

The following is written to the Church in Laodicea:

"And to the angel of the church in Laodicea write: 'The words of the Amen, the faithful and true witness, the beginning of God's creation.

*I know your works: you are neither cold nor hot. Would that you were either cold or hot! So, because you are lukewarm, and neither hot nor cold, I will spit you out of my mouth. **For you say, I am rich, I have prospered, and I need nothing**, not realizing that you are wretched, pitiable, poor, **blind**, and naked. **I counsel you to buy from me** gold refined by fire, so that you may be rich, and white garments so that you may clothe yourself and the shame of your nakedness may not be seen, **and salve to anoint your eyes, so that you may see**. Those whom I love, I reprove and discipline, **so be zealous and repent**."* REVELATION 3:14-19 (ESV, emphases mine)

How do we "buy" salve from God to heal our blindness? Revelation 3:19 tells us — "Repentance" is God's redemptive and restorative currency!

Unrepentant sin is like a cataract on our spiritual vision and Christianity has had blinding spiritual cataracts in regard to the Jewish people for its entire history as evidenced by Paul's strong exhortation in Romans 11 to the nascent "church":

> *"For I would not, brethren, that ye should be ignorant of this mystery, lest ye should be **wise in your own conceits**; that blindness in part is happened to Israel, until the fullness of the Gentiles be come in."* ROMANS 11:25 (KJV, emphasis mine)

We can be quick to call out the blinding of Israel in this verse, but in doing that we demonstrate that we are blinded ourselves in ignorance and haughtiness (wise in our own conceits) because any blinding that there is, is actually due to us — it's for our sake. This fact should give us a heart of gratefulness and compassion, not judgment and persecution.

But that has not been the case. Where does our own blinding come from?

From my own experience, I was very ignorant of the horrific and relentless Christian persecution of the Jewish People. This relentless persecution is just a symptom of a corrupt root of Replacement Theology that has been woven into our core beliefs and passed down in every generation for 2,000 years, as can be seen in The LIST.

We are stewed and marinated in Replacement Theology, and as such, are prone to embrace it unwittingly. So much so, that most Christians have no clue that Martin Luther, the "Father of the Reformation," so influential and revered in Christianity, was horrifically antisemitic (*see entries on The LIST: 1538, 1543*). His words and sentiments fueled the climate and atmosphere for the Holocaust. I can promise you that the Jewish people are painfully aware of this at great cost.

Martin Luther was German and lived in Germany. In *Mein Kampf*, Hitler credits him as a great German hero. Starting with the year 1543, The LIST shows some of the shockingly direct connections between Luther and Hitler:

- Martin Luther writes *On The Jews and Their Lies, 1543* — where he actually lays out the foundational blueprint for the Holocaust, all in the name of Christ.

- *Kristallnacht* Pogroms in Germany on November 9-10, 1938 — celebrated ON Martin Luther's birthday, November 10th! This shows a DIRECT connection between the *Kristallnacht* tragedy, WHO the Nazis were remembering and honoring, and WHERE they got their ideas from to do such evil.

- The HOLOCAUST 1939-45 — the Final Solution is executed in Germany with much credit given to Martin Luther's views and recommendations in treatment of the Jewish people, exactly 400 years after *On The Jews and Their Lies* was written.

It was heartbreaking to learn that the "Father of the Reformation" – who had the truly magnificent revelation of "righteousness by faith and faith alone" was so antisemitic that he couldn't apply that amazing revelation to God's chosen people, in complete contradiction of the following scriptures:

"And the scripture was fulfilled which say, Abraham believed God, and it was imputed unto him for righteousness: and he was called the Friend of God." JAMES 2:23 (KJV)

God calls the children of Israel "The apple of His Eye" in Zechariah 2 with a warning:

"For thus saith the LORD of hosts; After the glory hath he sent me unto the nations which spoiled you: for he that touches you touches the apple of his eye." ZECHARIAH 2:8 (KJV)

Martin Luther planted a toxic black seed of antisemitism into our Protestant religion that we are still under the influence of today. This is demonstrated in:

- not being aware of this, we are blind to it, and

- continuing attitudes towards the Jewish people decreeing that the faith of Abraham is not righteous, exhibited in terminology we use. For example calling them "non-believers" in direct contradiction to James 2:23, Romans 4:3 and Galatians 3:6.

   For what saith the scripture? Abraham believed God and it was counted unto him for righteousness. ROMANS 4:3 (KJV)

Some time ago the LORD reprimanded me forcefully, and I heard "Don't you dare call them non-believers. You believe **because** they believe" – they are the original believers, not us. I realized that in this attitude we are judging them - The apple of God's eye - and ourselves, and I had to repent.

When we Christians speak among ourselves about those who do not believe in Yeshua, it is common for us to refer to all such people as *unbelievers*. But Jews consider themselves - and in fact are - the *original* believers in the God of Abraham, Isaac, and Jacob. Like Abraham, they believe God's Word is true! Therefore, regarding the Jewish people, I have come to agree with God and His word and believe it is wrong for Christians to ever call Jews *unbelievers*.

This blinding remains in place until we own the sin of our Church forefathers and our own sin in regard to our Jewish brethren.

Thankfully, wherever we find ourselves caught in a trap, God always provides a way out. In Leviticus 26:40-42 a loving God tells "The apple of His eye" that when they find themselves suffering under the curses of unrepented sin, not just their own, but of their ancestors, as well, here is what we need to do:

> *"If they shall confess their iniquity, and the iniquity of their fathers, with their trespass which they trespassed against me, and that also they have walked contrary unto me; And that I also have walked contrary unto them, and have brought them into the land of their enemies; if then their uncircumcised hearts be humbled, and they then accept of the punishment of their iniquity: Then will I remember my covenant with Jacob, and also my covenant with Isaac, and also my covenant with Abraham will I remember; and I will remember the land."* LEVITICUS 26:40-42 (KJV)

If we curse the children of Israel without repenting, we heap curses upon ourselves AND our children… and that is what many in the church are suffering from today. We can never become a glorious church without spot or blemish, as long as we don't repent for our horrific history towards "The apple of God's eye" that has repeated in EVERY generation since Yeshua walked the earth – and that we are doomed to repeat if we don't repent and turn, which in Hebrew is *teshuvah*.

We can rejoice in the same way that God provided a way of restoration to the nation of Israel, we can also be restored, no matter how blind we have been or how many generations have erred! How good is our God!

Thank You that You are such a good God! And, that You have a good plan laid out before the foundation of the earth with Your beloved Jewish people in the center of that plan.

Thank You for choosing the Jewish people as Your vessel to make Yourself known among the nations. I acknowledge that I wouldn't know You, Your Word or Your salvation without the Jewish people. Thank You that even though our spiritual ancestors have horribly treated them, Your mercies are new every day.

Will you pray this repentance prayer with me?

Avinu shebashamayim, our Father in Heaven, thank You that You provide a way to buy salve to remove the blinding cataracts/scales and restore our sight. Father, we confess to You and repent of the antisemitic sins of our Church forefathers that have led to such relentless, horrific, murderous persecutions in Your name. We also confess and repent of our own spiritual ignorance and arrogance that has led us into any thoughts of Replacement Theology or antisemitism.

Continue to break our heart for what breaks Your heart. Continue to heal our spiritual blindness and show us how to truly comfort Your people. Help us to see "The apple of Your eye" with Your eyes of love and tender mercy.

Thank You that we live in a day to see Your purposes for Your people come to pass before our very eyes, and that we can be a part of that.

In the name of the God of Abraham, Isaac and Jacob/Israel — *Am Yisrael Chai!* The people of Israel Live!!! The Time to Favor Zion has come, HALLELUJAH!

Baruch HaShem / Blessed be The Name of The Lord.

The "Jew Sow" in Wittenberg

by Sister Joela

"You worship what you do not know; we know what we worship, for salvation is of the Jews." JOHN 4:22 (NKJV)

When you walk into the church where Martin Luther once preached, you will see the God of Israel and Jesus the King of the Jews being worshipped and honored. On the outside wall of the same church He is being mocked and cast aspersions on, together with His people.

Pictured above: Judensau stone carving on the Wittenberg church where Martin Luther attended.

There you can see a stone sculpture of a sow, which had been made with the intention to deter Jews from making their home in Wittenberg. This was placed high upon the church wall in 1305 and has remained there ever since (*see entry on The LIST, 1305*).

Above the relief is a golden inscription with the words "Rabini Schem Hamphoras", the "Rabbinic name for the 'unknowable name' of God".

It was written in 1570, some years after Luther's passing, and quotes the title of his worst anti-Jewish writing, *Von Schem Hamphoras und vom Geschlecht Christi:* "Of the Unknowable Name and the Generations of Christ", published in 1543 (*see entry on The LIST, 1543*), where he wrote a comment about that mocking sculpture upon his church – it is full of hatred and truly insulting:

> *"Here in Wittenberg, in our parish church, there is a sow carved into the stone under which lie young pigs and Jews who are sucking; behind the sow stands a rabbi who is lifting up the right leg of the sow, raises behind the sow, bows down and looks with great effort into the Talmud under the sow, as if he wanted to read and see something most difficult and exceptional; no doubt they gained their Shem Hamphoras* [the 'unknowable name' of God] *from that place..."*

Hardly anyone is aware of the fact that in these golden Letters the Holy Name, *"Ha Shem"* is hidden.

Preparations for the 500th anniversary of the Reformation had been underway for many years. It would have been such a great chance to remove this obscene, blasphemous, scoffing sculpture as a sign of repentance and reconciliation for all the world to see. But it did not happen (*see entry on The LIST, 2016*).

When I began considering the matter in 2013 and doing research on it, a burning desire grew in my heart that it would be removed, and I deeply hoped that a person of public interest would do that.

In the beginning, I was not too excited to enter into this battle. I knew it was costly and the chances for success were limited. Martin Luther's church is also a UNESCO world heritage site! I must confess that my love for God is often too weak a flame to get me moving. But for people without a deep relationship to God it is even harder. Their human logic and reasoning gets in the way and excuses are made. In the end, a decision was made NOT to remove the stone sow from the Wittenberg church:

> *"To date [22nd of June 2016] the Parish Church Council stands by the decision to retain a culture of remembrance with a visible defamatory sculpture in its original position. In our experience direct exposure helps people to face up to and concern themselves with the past. It is our desire that this form of remembrance should have a formative effect on historical awareness and should be respected."*[1]

So the sanctification of His Name and the love for His people on the one side is opposed by our politics and culture of remembrance on the other side, a culture we have become proud of because it salves our conscience.

This "No" remained being a "No" even after much support by international believers, after a petition was signed by nearly 10,000 people, and after prayer vigils on the central Market Square. The only tangible success was that papers from the *Jerusalem Post to Christianity Today* as well as local broadcasts made the issue public and well-known.

God's ways are perfect. Originally I opposed the suggestion that we could speak in that church during our final "Wittenberg 2017 Repentance and Prayer Conference"; even more when I heard it was my turn to speak. THAT church of all places!

But with time I began to understand: repentance has to go from the inside to the outside. What could be better than asking for forgiveness from inside this very church, in unity with kindred brothers and sisters?

God added His "Yes and Amen", last but not least, through a Jewish woman from Ukraine, who happened to be in the church at the time of the speech. She came to thank us and she was deeply moved.

Has this been the punch line? No, this matter is still ongoing — not as expected, though. During our many prayer vigils we got to know a Jewish man who decided to take the matter to court. A brilliant lawyer from the Wittenberg 2017 initiative filed the suit which will be heard on April 4, 2019 in Dessau.

God has striven for the honor of His Name throughout the ages. Again and again He spared, warned, gave grace — but also gave judgment. He will answer at His time — for the sake of the Glory of His Name.

Will you pray this repentance prayer with me?

Our Father, holy, eternal, almighty God,

Please forgive us when we are unwilling to fight for Your Honor, which in fact is such a privilege. Our love for You is so often only like a smoldering wick, and only Your grace keeps the little flame alive. How often we pray "Hallowed be Your Name", and pray a formal prayer only, while our hearts are divided. Your law warns about misusing Your Name, but we can so easily take it lightly. We do not see how serious Your judgment is, and that we are responsible to warn our neighbor. Have mercy on us who have lost our fear of God and have forgotten that You are a consuming Flame.

Forgive the blindness of our deep self-righteousness. We are guilty that the ancient words chiseled in stone still have the power to insult. Forgive our indifference against the wounds these ongoing insults cut into the hearts of Your people. Forgive our excuses, pretending a plaque in the ground could be sufficient.

Forgive us, for while our mouth says "Never again", at the same time our passivity and indifference allows the identical sin to continue on and on.

For 700 years You have been bearing this public scorn, the hatred of Jews carved in stone, while we discuss whether we should clear these "shouting stones" off.

O soften our hearts of stone, soften them for Your suffering and for the suffering of Your people!

Amen.

ENDNOTES:

1. Dr. Johannes Block for the Church Council for the *Evangelische Stadtkirchengemeinde* (Protestant Church Parish), Wittenberg.

Are We Cut Off?

by Bob O'Dell

In his letter to the followers of Jesus in the 1st century church in Rome, Paul sternly warns the Gentiles about proper relationship to all Jews, when he says:

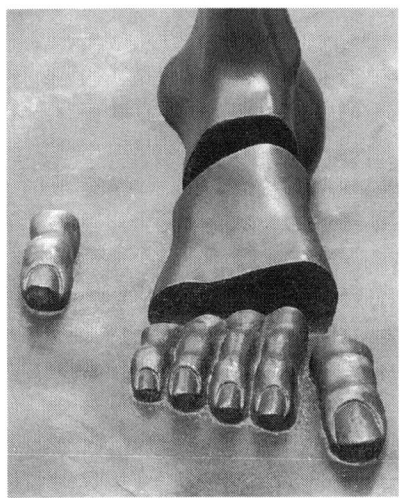

"If some of the branches have been broken off, and you, though a wild olive shoot, have been grafted in among the others and now share in the nourishing sap from the olive root, do not consider yourself to be superior to those other branches. If you do, consider this: You do not support the root, but the root supports you. You will say then, "Branches were broken off so that I could be grafted in." Granted. But they were broken off because of unbelief, and you stand by faith. Do not be arrogant, but tremble. For if God did not spare the natural branches, he will not spare you either. Consider therefore the kindness and sternness of God: sternness to those who fell, but kindness to you, provided that you continue in his kindness. Otherwise, you also will be cut off." ROMANS 11:17-22 (NIV)

Pictured left: Foot that is "cut off".

What are the instructions we are given in these verses?

1. **Do not consider yourself superior to those other branches.** In other words, do not consider our life with God, our Christian expressions of life, to be superior to those other branches, the Jewish branches that have been broken off!

2. **Do not be arrogant but tremble.** In other words, do not be arrogant against the Jewish people because you have been grafted in, and they have been broken off.

3. **Consider the kindness and sternness of God.** In other words, actively think about how kind God has been to us as Gentiles and how stern God has been to the Jews. Paul is asking us to take those things to heart and let them be worked into our hearts in the right way!

4. **Continue in his kindness.** In other words, because we have received God's kindness, we need to act and behave in a manner consistent with that kindness, as evidenced by the quality of our relationship with the Jewish branches.

Now let us honestly ask ourselves the following four questions.

1. Did the Church historically refrain from considering itself superior to those other branches? **The answer is NO!**

2. Did the Church refrain from being arrogant and did the Church tremble before God? **The answer is clearly NO!**

3. Did the Church consider the kindness and the sternness of God, and let those truths guide us to walk properly before God? Our record of actions towards the Jewish people for centuries culminating in the Holocaust would answer **NO!**

4. Did the Church continue in His kindness with respect to the Jewish people? **The answer is clearly NO!**

Then what does Paul tell us will happen according to these verses?

1. For if God did not spare the natural branches, He **will not spare** you either.

2. Otherwise, you also will be **cut off.**

What in the world does it mean that we will not be spared? What in the world does it mean that we will also be "cut off"? The vast majority of Christians, if they have ever read them, believe that these verses are still only a warning. But are they?

After my experience with the 9th of Av in 2013, and after realizing how ugly our history with the Jews was, I began to study the concept of being cut off. I found some who teach these verses as a warning about how easily we can lose our salvation. I think that is an excessive interpretation. In the Mosaic law, being cut off did not mean you were sold into slavery, sent back to Egypt, or killed. Yet it was not wimpy either. It meant that you were forced to pitch your tent outside the main camp for a very long time, and your rights to participate in normal community life were severed.

The New Testament parable of the ten virgins in Matthew 25 also illustrates being cut off. All ten virgins slept and were awakened by the coming of the bridegroom, but only five were wise enough to have "additional reserves" of oil with them. The others were foolish. I don't see this parable as describing the saved versus the unsaved, because all are virgins. It is about a difference in perspective and preparedness amongst the saved. As a result, only five would have the honor of being able to attend the great wedding banquet. The other five were literally "cut off" from the wedding banquet, being close enough to be heard when they cried out, yet not granted permission to enter.

One day, while I was again considering this warning from Paul, and what it could mean for us, I found the courage to ask God about it directly:

"LORD, what would being cut-off look like, if it were to ever happen to us?"

I felt that God immediately answered me right back with a question of His own:

"What makes you think it hasn't already happened?"

Now that caught me by surprise. And so I began to consider a new question, *"What has already happened around us that has caused us to be "cut off"?* Today I will share with you one of several answers to that question, that I have come to see.

Stop and look around. Do you not see an assault on Christianity at every turn? Church attendance is down. Thousands of churches are closing each year in the United States. Meanwhile, the fastest growing category in the religious surveys are the "nothings" who are people who don't believe in anything.

The greatest enemy of the Church in the Western world today is *secularism*. It is anti-God, anti-Christ, anti-Christian, anti-Judaism, and anti-Israel. Our

Christian expression, our liberty and freedom of speech, is under assault by secularism. Its aim? To *cut us off* from any public, community-wide expression of our beliefs. Maybe we can pray indoors, but we must not take any action outside our homes that even hints at advancing our views in society. In short, they want us to be cut off from our own society, our own nations.

What then, is the origin of this great enemy of our time: secularism? We read about it in The LIST in the year 1670:

> *"Calvinist Synod of Northern Holland bans Spinoza's work which later on inspires The Enlightenment.*
>
> *Specifically Theologico-Political Treatise. Baruch Spinoza's writings would later be credited with laying the groundwork of the 18th Century Enlightenment (emphasizing the physical alone -- 'If you can't see it, it doesn't exist'), a movement which would in turn be extended by others into secular humanism, socialism and Marxism. In addition Spinoza is credited with laying the groundwork for modern biblical criticism that challenges the divine inspiration of the Bible. While Spinoza, a Jew, is disparaged by Christians today for his atheism and for having inspired Marxism, a question we (the compilers of this list) see being ignored is the degree to which the ongoing Inquisitions of the Church, with their inherent irrationality and brutality, may have propelled Spinoza to envision a world that exists without God. Did we, the Church, create through Spinoza that great enemy which today stands in opposition to our Judeo-Christian values? Did we, the Church, sow 'the Inquisitions' and reap 'secular humanism'?"*

When the Church had complete power, it could not resist the evil inclination to persecute the Jewish people, and demean them for any practice of Judaism. These Inquisitions literally and emotionally sucked the life out of the Jewish people. Eleven years earlier, in 1659, Baruch Spinoza (a Jew) was himself investigated by the Spanish Inquisition. Spinoza's own family had previously left Portugal for Holland to escape the Inquisitions!

In the face of countless atrocities under the title: *Inquisition*, something had to break loose. His name was Spinoza. He questioned the goodness of God, and even the existence of God. Shunned by the Church through the Inquisitions, and then expelled by his synagogue for his atheism, Spinoza envisioned a world that might exist without God. Spinoza would become a hero of secular movements, eventually credited with laying the groundwork for the 18th Century Enlightenment, and then would have his own thoughts extended by others into secular humanism, socialism and Marxism.

We Christians are right now being cut off from our own nations by the still growing ranks of the secularists. And it was the multitude of sins that the Church committed against Jews that I believe **was the catalyst** for secularism in the first place.

Will you pray this repentance prayer with me?

Father in Heaven,

What shall we do? Have our forefathers sinned before you, and are we reaping the sin of the Inquisition in the form of secularism? Are we being cut off from our own nations?

Give us eyes to see the truth! Is this the truth? Allow us to come to terms with the sins of our past and the impact that the sins of the Church have had on society today.

Oh, Lord, what shall we do? How shall we respond to the possibility that we have launched a great attack upon ourselves by our own sins of the past? Can this reaping be fixed? Can this reaping be undone? Can we fast, pray and repent our way out of this predicament? What shall we do?

Father, we know that regardless of the crisis in which we find ourselves, You encourage us to cry out to You and plead for forgiveness. It is never too late to seek Your mercy! You say that when we truly repent before You, that You will answer us! Lead us and guide us in that process. Hear our prayers! Forgive us and our forefathers, we do pray!

In Yeshua's name, we pray.

Amen.

His Light is Shining from Zion — Get Ready!

By Nathalie Blackham

The LIST is a monumental and thoroughly researched work and exposes the sins of our Church forefathers. After reading through The LIST, we see that the ugly tentacles of antisemitism are not in one country but have spread all over the world.

Sadly, I am personally familiar with the long history of antisemitism in France, and would like to reflect with you about the "Dreyfus Affair" (*see entry on The LIST, 1894*).

First let me give you a bit of historical background. The Dreyfus scandal began in December 1894 when Captain Alfred Dreyfus was convicted of treason. Dreyfus was a young French Jewish artillery officer. He was sentenced to life imprisonment for allegedly communicating French military secrets to the German Embassy in Paris. Dreyfus was imprisoned for five years on Devil's Island in French Guiana.

In 1896, new evidence came to light that Dreyfus was actually innocent. Georges Picquart, head of counter-espionage, identified a French Army major, Ferdinand Walsin Esterhazy, as the true culprit. After high-ranking military officials suppressed the new evidence, a military court unanimously acquitted Esterhazy in a kangaroo court trial that lasted only two days.

The Army then accused Dreyfus with additional charges based on falsified documents.

Pictured above: Cover of Le Petit Journal covering the Dreyfus Affair, France 1894.

Word of the military court's framing of Dreyfus and of the attempted cover-up began to spread, chiefly owing to *J'Accuse...!*, a vehement open letter[1] published in a Paris newspaper in January 1898 by writer Émile Zola.[2] Activists put pressure on the government to reopen the case.

In 1899, Dreyfus was returned to France for another trial. The intense political and judicial scandal that ensued divided French society between those who supported Dreyfus (now called "Dreyfusards") and those who condemned him (the "anti-Dreyfusards"), including Édouard Drumont, director and publisher of the antisemitic newspaper, *La Libre Parole*.[3]

The new trial resulted in another conviction and a 10-year sentence. Dreyfus was later given a pardon and set free. Eventually all the accusations against Dreyfus were demonstrated to be baseless.

Theodor Herzl, the modern day "Father of Zionism," watched all of these injustices happening to Jewish Officer Dreyfus, which is what inspired him to write "A Modern Solution to the Jewish Question,"[4] which casts the vision for a Jewish homeland.

Enough of the historical background. Now let me get personal.

One day, I discovered a letter in our old family recipe book. We know the recipient of the letter was Édouard Drumont, the publisher of the antisemitic newspaper, *La Libre Parole*, founded in 1892. The letter is dated 30th January 1894, which is the year of the Dreyfus Affair. Here is part of the letter:

The letter begins:

"Mon Cher Monsieur Drumond,

Je lis assidûment la Libre Parole et je suis de tout coeur avec vous dans la lutte que vous avez entreprise contre les Juifs. Vous avez mille fois raison de prouver à tous qu'ils nous envahissent de toutes parts. Comme vous le démontrez si bien, tous les bons emplois sont pour eux, les grandes terres passent peu à peu entre leurs mains, et si l'on n'y met bon ordre ils finiront par accaparer toute la fortune de la France. Vous, Monsieur, dont l'esprit est si fertile, ne sauriez vous trouver un moyen d'empêcher un pareil malheur et de faire..."

Translated into English, it reads as follow:

"My dear Mr. Drummond,

I read la Libre Parole eagerly, I am wholeheartedly with you in the struggle you have against the Jews. As you

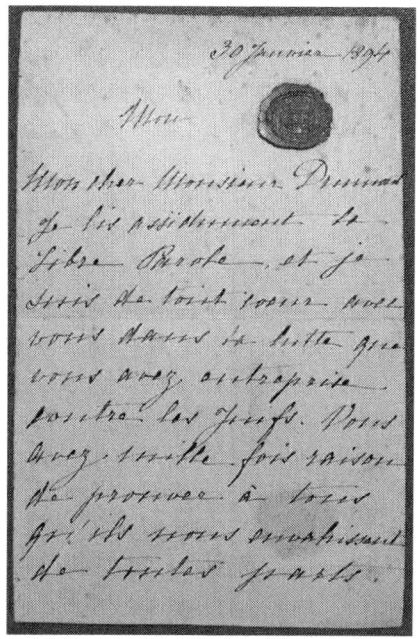

Pictured above: Screenshot of the first page of the original letter found in the family cookbook. Used with permission.

show so well, all good jobs are for them (The Jews), the big lands gradually passing in their hands and if we do not put order they will eventually seize all the fortunes of France. You, Sir, whose spirit is so fertile, can find a way to prevent such a misfortune..."

I come from one of the oldest French aristocratic, Catholic families. I remember my mother telling me that when she was going to Mass on Good Friday, they were praying against their enemies, the Jews! This was just after World War II. She confessed to me: "In my heart of a child, I felt pain to pray such a prayer!"

My parents visited Israel in 1980, and my dad, not a man of many words said, "I will make sure that all my children will visit this land." I started to pray for Israel around that time. At the time, I was 19 years old, and my diaries are full of entries praying for Israel. At the time, I did not know very much about this beautiful country.

Fast forward 40 years...

Now in Israel, my husband and I are producing a weekly TV program entitled, Israel First! We interview Jewish people to speak about the goodness of Israel and we help to export the wisdom of the Torah to the nations. We are humbly doing that work, knowing that we are part of a Great Awakening.

The nations are ready to receive the light of Zion as it is written in Isaiah 2:2-5:

> *"And it shall come to pass in the last days, that the mountain of the* Lord's *house shall be established in the top of the mountains, and shall be exalted above the hills; and all nations shall flow unto it. And many people shall go and say, Come ye, and let us go up to the mountain of the* Lord, *to the house of the God of Jacob; and he will teach us of his ways, and we will walk in his paths: for out of Zion shall go forth the law (Torah), and the word of the* Lord *from Jerusalem. And he shall judge among the nations, and shall rebuke many people: and they shall beat their swords into plowshares, and their spears into pruning hooks: nation shall not lift up sword against nation, neither shall they learn war any more. O house of Jacob, come ye, and let us walk in the light of the* Lord. *"* (KJV)

We have been educated with a deep and long seated antisemitism in the Church. There are many false concepts that pervade our seminaries, bible colleges and Christian schools. We have broken our connection with the teaching of the Torah and severed ties with the Jewish community.

Now that we realise how far we have fallen, we need to ask for forgiveness from our Father in heaven and also on earth to our Jewish friends. There have been so many atrocities perpetrated by our Church forefathers through the ages due to false teachings and wrong interpretations.

We need to repent. The word repent, in Hebrew, is *teshuvah*, and it means to return. We need to reconnect with the Jewish community and we need to reconnect with the Torah, the powerful Word of God given by the God of Israel. It is the greatest gift to humanity!

Will you pray this repentance prayer with me?

Abba, I am so so sorry for what my family was involved in during the Dreyfus Affair in France. Thank You for letting me find this letter in a family cookbook. I stand in the gap and ask for Your forgiveness on behalf of my ancestors who participated in the treachery done against Captain Alfred Dreyfus.

Thank You for giving many Christians a heart for Israel and her people. In our case, it is a privilege to serve them in their land and bring news from the heart of the world.

We mourn together for all the Jewish people who had their lives cut short, and who suffered under the hands of the Christian community through the last two millennia. We mourn for the Jews who were dragged to courts and killed for their faith. We cry for the unrighteous deeds perpetrated by the governments of our nations. We repent of the blindness of our religious leaders who did not want to learn Torah with our Jewish friends who brought the Word of God to humanity.

We pray that we will honor Jewish communities around the world, that we will respect them, stand with them in times of distress, and do our utmost to serve them to share the Light of the Torah to the nations.

In Jesus' name,

Amen.

ENDNOTES:

1. https://en.wikipedia.org/wiki/Open_letter

2. https://en.wikipedia.org/wiki/%C3%89mile_Zola

3. https://en.wikipedia.org/wiki/La_Libre_Parole

4. https://archive.org/details/cu31924028579781/page/n51

Perpetrators, Collaborators and Enablers

by Steve Wearp

"Silence in the face of evil is itself evil: God will not hold us guiltless. Not to speak is to speak. Not to act is to act." attributed to Dietrich Bonhoeffer[1], German pastor, theologian, and anti-Nazi dissident

For most of us, the Holocaust was a repulsive event committed against the Jews by the Nazis during World War II. We also assume that the morally superior allied forces fought and saved the Jewish people from the Nazi death camps. Thus, we conveniently exclude ourselves and our Church forefathers from knowledge and responsibility for the extermination of six million Jews. The question is — are the nations truly innocent, or are our hands also stained with blood?

Between 1933 and 1939, the Nazi regime imposed over 400 laws stripping its Jewish subjects of the most basic of human rights, property, businesses and dignity.[2] The Jews in Germany and Austria were no longer citizens, but state subjects without rights or due process.

The year is 1938, the Nuremberg laws are in force throughout Germany and Austria, and the Jewish people have been systematically oppressed by the Nazi regime. Responding to increasing political pressure, President Roosevelt called for a meeting of the nations to determine a course of action to deal with the Jewish crisis in Germany and Austria.

In July of 1938, the United States, Great Britain, France, Canada and 28 other nations gathered in Évian, France (*see entry on The LIST, Évian Conference, 1938*). They were joined by dozens of humanitarian organizations and hundreds of reporters from around the world to discuss the "Jewish Refugee Problem".

President Roosevelt chose to send a personal friend, Myron C. Taylor as the US representative[3] instead of a US State Department representative, rendering any statement he might make as an "advisory" comment, holding no binding power.

The British received a mandate from the League of Nations in 1923 to oversee the creation of a Jewish homeland in Palestine, but they refused to allow Jewish immigration due to the ongoing Arab & Jewish conflict. The United States delegate said this was a matter for Congress to decide, and that he was powerless to make any commitment, while the French claimed they had already done more than their fair share.

The Canadian Prime Minister noted in his diary that *"We must . . . seek to keep this part of the Continent free from unrest and from too great an intermixture of foreign strains of blood." In his view, nothing was to be gained "by creating an internal problem in an effort to meet an international one."*[4]

One by one, the rest of the nations came forth and stated their positions. Nicaragua, Costa Rica, Honduras, and Panama stated that they wanted no traders or intellectuals — code words for Jews. Argentina said it had already accommodated enough immigrants from Central Europe. Canada cited its unemployment problem. Australia said that it had no "racial problems" and did not want to create any by bringing in Jewish refugees. Imperial countries such as Britain, France, and the Netherlands said that their tropical territories offered only limited prospects for European refugees. The League of Nations High Commissioner Sir Neill Malcolm was openly hostile to the idea of a new refugee organization.[4]

Hitler and the Nazi regime had their answer: no one wanted the Jews, and the nations of the world were not interested in opposing their anti-Jewish policies.

✿ ✿ ✿   Three Months Later   ✿ ✿ ✿

Kristallnacht, November 9ᵗʰ-10ᵗʰ, 1938 (*see entry on The LIST, Nov 9-10, 1938*)

The consequences of all the nations of the world refusing to act was realized — innocence was lost. The illusion of civility and culture that Europe, the United States and the world thought they had attained was exposed as hypocrisy.

The hearts of all nations were laid bare through a brazen demonstration by the Nazi regime to systematically destroy the Jewish people. This was a day that witnessed the destruction of hundreds of synagogues and thousands of businesses. This was a day when thirty thousand innocent Jewish people were sent to concentration camps and hundreds more were murdered by paramilitary & civilians in Austria and Germany:[5]

- 7,000+ Jewish Shops, Stores and Businesses ransacked, burned and pillaged, and storefront windows shattered (Night of Broken Glass)

- 1,400+ Synagogues and Yeshiva's destroyed, burned and desecrated.

- 30,000 Jewish men arrested and taken to concentration camps at Dachau, Buchenwald, and Sachsenhausen.

- 91+ Jews murdered and thousands beaten and humiliated in their homes and on the streets.

This took place in the very heartland of Christian Europe, the bastion of the Reformation and the center for protestant theology. All this without even a whimper from the pulpits, let alone from the Church as an institution — the only sound heard was the deafening silence.

Will you pray this repentance prayer with me?

Father forgive us and have mercy upon us for we have willfully sinned against You and the Jewish people, whom You chose to bear Your name.

Pictured above: Clean up after Kristallnacht.

Father forgive us and have mercy upon us for we sat in silence as the Jews were persecuted, maligned, mistreated and murdered.

Father forgive us and have mercy upon us for we were collaborators with those who hated them and willingly turned them over for destruction.

Father forgive us and have mercy upon us for we raised our hands to strike and slaughter them without mercy.

Father forgive us and have mercy upon us for our hands are stained with the blood of your Saints, the children of Israel:

~ their only crime was that they were called by Your Name ~

Father forgive us and have mercy upon us for our arrogance and pride when we falsely proclaimed that we were chosen above Israel.

Father allow us, your humble servants to bring healing and hope, blessing and honor, joy and peace to your people Israel. May they know Your love through our repentance, service and sacrificial hearts.

Amen.

ENDNOTES:

1. https://en.wikiquote.org/wiki/Dietrich_Bonhoeffer

2. https://encyclopedia.ushmm.org/content/en/article/antisemitic-legislation-1933-1939

3. https://newspapers.ushmm.org/events/evian-conference-offers-neither-help-nor-haven

4. https://www.facinghistory.org/resource-library/evian-conference

5. https://en.wikipedia.org/wiki/Kristallnacht

Breaking Glass

by Linda Chandler

As a solo pastor of a Christian Church, I am very cognizant of being a doorkeeper of one of God's houses; I am mindful of the tremendous responsibility of shepherding God's flock according to God's will and commands.

For me, Kristallnacht, the Night of Broken Glass on November 9-10, 1938 is a nightmare for any "doorkeeper of God's house" (*see entry on The LIST, Nov 9-10, 1938*). How did this horror happen? 267 synagogues were broken into and burned while 7,000 stores were looted, all to the sound of smashing glass. At least 91 Jews were murdered on that fateful night. Where were the Christian pastors who knew the sanctity and responsibility of a house of God? Yes, these were Jewish "houses of God," but the root of our Christian faith and salvation is from the "Jewish" Son of God, Jesus.

As I meditate on "how" this travesty happened, I learned that the hammers used to break the glass were 400-year old words taken from a document entitled "On the Jews and Their Lies".[1]

This document was used by the Nazis to perpetuate hatred of the Jews which then birthed this night of horror. Here is a quote from this document which became the template for the "Night of Broken Glass":

> *"What shall we Christians do with this rejected and condemned people, the Jews? Since they live among us, we dare not tolerate their conduct, now that*

we are aware of their lying and reviling and blaspheming. If we do, we become sharers in their lies, cursing and blasphemy...

I shall give you my sincere advice:

First to set fire to their synagogues or schools and to bury and cover with dirt whatever will not burn, so that no man will ever again see a stone or cinder of them. This is to be done in honor of our LORD and of Christendom, so that God might see that we are Christians, and do not condone or knowingly tolerate such public lying, cursing and blaspheming of his Son and of his Christians.

Second, I advise that their houses also be razed and destroyed. For they pursue in the same aims as in their synagogues..."[2]

Pictured above: Kristallnacht, Night of broken glass, November 9, 1938.

The Nazis even picked the dates for "Kristallnacht" (November 9-10, 1938) to coincide with Martin Luther's birthday (November 10) in order to advance the nightmare. Martin Luther, who led the Protestant Reformation first with these words, *"by faith alone we are saved"* (Habakkuk 2:4), forgot that his faith came from Jesus, a Jew, who taught *"...salvation comes from the Jews"* (John 4:22), and he went on to write this deceitful and destructive document.

The negative thoughts penned by Martin Luther were used to shatter hundreds of glass windows 400 years later. My stomach turns and my heart cries to see how a person's words can literally cut like glass into our future and bleed out the tenets of our faith, causing terror, mayhem, and loss of life.

But no man or nation or words can stand against Our Living God forever. Eric Metaxas, in his biography of Dietrich Bonhoeffer wrote:[3]

> *"Bonhoeffer often spoke of Jesus Christ as the 'man for others,' as selflessness incarnate, loving and serving others to the absolute exclusion of his needs and desires. Similarly, the church of Jesus Christ existed for 'others.' And since Christ was the LORD over the whole world, not just the church, the church existed to reach out beyond itself, to speak out for the voiceless, to defend the weak and fatherless. In 1938, Bonhoeffer's views on this subject were particularly sharpened as a result of the disturbing event of November 9. It was now, for the first time, that his gaze was in a new way directed away from his own trials and toward the trials of God's people, the Jews."*

The day after Kristallnacht, Bonhoeffer was reading and meditating on Psalm 74. Verse 8 grabbed his attention:

> *"They said in their hearts, Let us destroy them together: they have burned up all the synagogues of God in the land."* (KJV)

He underlined the verse and marked it further by drawing a line and making an exclamation point in the margin. Bonhoeffer next sent a circular letter to his young disciples he was teaching in the Finkenwalde community and pointed out this insight that *"the synagogues that had been burned in Germany were God's own"* and the connection God was making to him and the Christians in Germany was *"to lift one's hand against the Jews was to lift one's hand against God himself".*[4]

Bonhoeffer then reminded his disciples of Zechariah 2:8:

> *"For thus says the LORD of hosts: "He sent Me after glory, to the nations which plunder you; for he who touches you touches the apple of His eye."* (NKJ)

God was making it clear that God Himself was being attacked by the Nazis when they attacked His people. The Jews were God's beloved; they were not His enemies.

Bonhoeffer was given a mandate from God to help staunch this bleeding out of faith caused by the broken glass of antisemitism. Today, the lesson learned from Kristallnacht is that there is an enemy of God always ready to attack, maim and kill using words — like broken glass. We, as doorkeepers in God's house, must learn to recognize the stench of antisemitism that can come from people once respected and thought to carry truth.

Replacement Theology must be purged. Its antisemitic definition states *"the Jews are out and the Christians take their place"*. This is a huge shard of broken glass being used to cut out the very root of our faith, leaving the Church like a withering vine that bears no fruit and brings forth only sour wine.

So today I want to claim the lessons learned from Kristallnacht and reclaim the "Night of Broken Glass" by confessing and using Romans 8:28:

> *"And we know that all things work together for good to them that love God, to them who are the called according to his purpose."* (NKJV)

Finally I want to repent for the Christian "houses of God" that failed to see the damage being done and that failed to "honor and protect" our Jewish roots.

There is a well-known Jewish symbol of "breaking a glass" at the end of a wedding ceremony. This custom dates back to a writing within the Talmud:

> *"Mar bar Rabina made a marriage feast for his son. He observed that the rabbis present were very gay. So he seized an expensive goblet worth 400 zuzim and broke it before them. Thus he made them sober."* (BERAKHOT 5:2)

Jewish thought demands that when there is rejoicing, there should be trembling. Interestingly, during the Middle Ages, synagogue facades in Germany were inlaid with a special stone for the express purpose of smashing a glass at the end of weddings. Later, the breaking of the glass was viewed as a reminder of the destruction of the Temple in Jerusalem. The Jewish lesson is that even at the height of personal joy, we recall the pain and losses suffered by the Jewish people and remember a world in need of healing.

The broken glass also suggests the frailty of human relationships. With the shattering of the glass a vow is recited: *"As this glass shatters, so may our marriage never break."* The institution of marriage comes from the Jewish biblical world view of covenant.

In Judaism a covenant was made by breaking or cutting something. Abraham made the first covenant with the Almighty by cutting animals in two. God sealed the covenant by passing between the halved pieces as a smoking pot and flaming torch, thus sealing the deal with His promise of being eternally present as Israel's protector and provider. Today at a Jewish wedding the broken glass is also thought of as "cutting the covenant" with God and sealing the two into one![5]

May we restore what was lost at Kristallnacht by smashing a glass and covenanting to never let our Jewish roots be taken from our vine of faith, for we are "echad" (one) with our Jewish brothers and sisters as God is "echad" (one)!

Will you pray this repentance prayer with me?

Please, Adonai, great and fearsome God, who keeps covenant and extends grace to those who love Him and who observe His commandments, hear this earnest prayer. We of the Christian faith have sinned, we have done wrong, we have acted wickedly, we have rebelled and cut off our Jewish roots that produced the Son You sent to save us. We have listened to beguiling voices that sought to destroy our trust in You and Your beloved children, the Jews, who You tell Your story through. To You, Almighty One, belongs righteousness, but to us today belongs shame for breaking faith in You and Your covenant plans to save ALL people! We call on Your compassion and ask for mercy and forgiveness for Kristallnacht and all other times we have erred on the side of human self-righteousness.

Adonai, in Your righteousness don't delay. For Your Name's Sake — bring healing and honor and restoration of relationship between Jews and Christians, so we may be One Kingdom under One King.

Amen and Amen.

Please note: The author of this devotion broke a glass to seal this confession. She invites any others who feel so led to do the same.

ENDNOTES:

1. https://www.jewishvirtuallibrary.org/martin-luther-quot-the-jews-and-their-lies-quot

2. Ibid.

3. Eric Metaxas, Bonhoeffer: Pastor, Martyr, Prophet, Spy, (Nashville TN, Thomas Nelson, 2010), 314-15

4. Ibid., 316

5. https://www.myjewishlearning.com/article/breaking-the-glass-at-a-jewish-wedding/

Is God Really With Us?

by Albert J. McCarn

We need museums to teach us what we do not know, and to reveal to us what we should have known. The Virginia War Museum in Newport News did that for me. This institution exists to educate the public about the American military experience, and to honor those who have borne the burdens of it. The exhibits cover every phase of my birth nation's conflicts, from the Revolutionary War to the Global War on Terrorism. As one might expect, many of those exhibits are devoted to World War II.

The disturbing thing about all wars, including World War II, is that they never bring permanent solutions to anything. The same evils overcome in one generation take shape again in the next, requiring renewed effort to keep them at bay. The evils overcome in the Great Patriotic War, as our erstwhile Soviet allies called it, were not foreign to us. They were, and remain, an integral part of the civilization the Allies struggled to preserve.

One exhibit made that abundantly clear to me. In a well-illuminated display case there hung the tunic of a German soldier. The buckle of the belt fastened around the tunic depicted an eagle of the Third Reich grasping in its claws the swastika of Hitler's National Socialist Party. That was not surprising, but the inscription above the eagle was a surprise. In capital letters it proclaimed boldly — GOTT MIT UNS.

"Gott mit uns" means "God with us." German soldiers have worn it on their uniforms for three centuries, long before the Prussian kings began uniting

the separate German states into the cohesive empire that eventually became the instrument of Nazi aggression. The Third Reich had ample reason to continue the tradition, not only for many of its soldiers, but also for certain civil servants.

Adolf Hitler, after all, believed he was doing the work of God in creating space for God's "master race" to rule the world. Such work required the

Pictured above: German belt buckle worn by Nazis.

enslavement or elimination of all those considered lesser beings according to Hitler's ideology: communists, homosexuals, Gypsies, Slavs…

…and especially Jews (*see entry on The LIST, 1933-45*).

Jews of Germany understood the inscription on the belts of police officers who enforced the decrees that robbed them of life, liberty, and property. Jews of Poland and Russia had no trouble deciphering *Gott mit uns* on the belts of soldiers who rounded them up and marched them away to an uncertain fate. Jews of France, Holland, Greece, and Italy would have recognized the message as Wehrmacht soldiers handed them off to *SS Totenkopf* (Death Head) units that staffed the camps where their lives became solitary, poor, nasty, brutish, and short.

What would those Jews have been thinking? Some surely wondered which god these Nazis thought was with them. That this was a Christian God seemed to be certain. The Germans were, after all, Christians. Protestants and Catholics alike embraced Nazism. Many of those same soldiers and policemen who efficiently eliminated 6,000,000 Jews faithfully attended church and chapel services, and almost all of them enjoyed the festivities of Christmas. The Christian God, then, was the one served by those who sought to make themselves masters of the earth over the bones of Jews and other supposedly lesser beings.

Why do we wonder that Jews have a hard time accepting the Christian message? If Christians — even nominal or cultural Christians — like the soldiers of the Third Reich did what they did in the belief that their crimes faithfully served their God, why would any Jew want to have anything to do with that God? If the experience of the *Shoah* (Holocaust) was the only evidence they had, then it follows that Jews might perceive the Jesus those German soldiers praised on Sunday must be a cruel god indeed, or perhaps a demon from hell.

Gott mit uns. God with us.

How arrogant. How dare they believe God would sanction such crimes? Surely the Nazi era was an anomaly. No other Christian nation would do such things. Surely none would believe that God's chosen people, the Jews, would be so deserving of His anger that they should be eliminated from the face of the earth. Surely the Germans were led astray. It could never happen to anyone else. Or could it? The sad truth is that the same refrain, "God with us," echoes throughout the corridors of history.

God with us —

— on the lips of Crusaders marching under the banner of the Cross, ravaging Jewish communities across Europe long before they ever set eyes on the Holy Land (*see entry on The LIST, 1096-1291*).

God with us —

— in the minds of Inquisition agents searching for Jewish homes in the cities of Spain. It was easy. Since the Torah prohibited Jews from kindling a flame on the Sabbath, all they had to do was wait until Saturday and look for the smokeless chimneys. Once identified, the Jews were given opportunity to embrace the Savior. If they refused, the best fate they might hope for would be deportation. Even descendants of Jews who converted were not immune. Those who aspired to a privileged position in society required a certificate of *limpieza de sangre* (purity of blood) to prove several generations of Christian heritage. Unwary applicants might find, to their horror, that they had a Jewish grandfather, making them subject to the mercies of the Inquisition courts (*see entry on The LIST, 1478-1834*).

God with us —

— in the decrees of Christian kings across Europe as they expelled Jews from their realms. Spain, England, France, Italy, Belgium, Switzerland, Hungary, Austria, Lithuania, Holland, Portugal, and the German states all did so (*see all entries beginning with "Jews expelled from" on The LIST in red*). After, of course, expropriating whatever Jewish wealth might be available to aid the crown in its "divine work."

God with us —

— moving the hands of Russian Orthodox magistrates as they authorized pogroms that made the Motherland uninhabitable for the Czar's Jewish subjects (*see entry on The LIST, 1881-1884*).

God with us —

> — in the hearts of American Protestants as they excluded Jews from their professional organizations and social clubs, insulted them with derisive jokes and demeaning names, and complained fearfully about Jewish bankers who supposedly controlled the world's wealth. It's not that these American Christians objected to the blessings of Jewish achievements. They appreciated the financial innovations of Marcus Goldman and Samuel Sachs, the scientific advances of Albert Einstein and J. Robert Oppenheimer, and the creativity of George Gershwin and Leonard Nimoy. It wasn't so bad that they were Jewish, but it would have been better if they could have been Jewish somewhere else.

Come to think of it, the German Nazi experience was not so unique after all. We might think of it more correctly as the culmination of two millennia of Christian holy arrogance. Such arrogance seems to have overlooked the solemn word of God:

> *"If the heavens above can be measured*
> *And the foundations of the earth searched out below,*
> *Then I will also cast off all the offspring of Israel*
> *For all that they have done,' declares the LORD."*
> JEREMIAH 31:37 (NASB)

If God can break His promises to the Jewish people, and to the rest of scattered Israel, then what prevents Him from breaking His promises to Christians? How, then, do we dare presume that we act for God by relegating Jews to the status of lesser human beings?

Or what do we make of these words of our Savior, the Messiah of Israel?

> *"They will make you outcasts from the synagogue, but an hour is coming for everyone who kills you to think that he is offering service to God. These things they will do because they have not known the Father or Me."* JOHN 16:2-3 (NASB)

It is customary to consider this as a prophecy of persecutions coming upon Christians, but we rarely consider that these words were spoken by a Jew to His Jewish disciples. Did He, perhaps, have in mind the persecutions that would happen to all His Father's covenant people, Jewish and non-Jewish alike?

Do we truly desire to heal this breach between Christians and Jews? The first thing we should do is to let our Heavenly Father restructure our thinking. It is, after all, His Kingdom we profess to serve. Perhaps He should have the last word about who is in it.

Will you pray this repentance prayer with me?

Our Father and our King,

Truly the revelation of Yeshua (Jesus) the Messiah is an awesome gift You have given. Your prophet Isaiah identifies Him as Immanuel: God With Us (Isaiah 7:14). The redemption of all Israel and the world through Him is the greatest message of life. Yet we who profess His Name have all too often turned the message "God with us" into an authorization to persecute those we should be embracing and honoring. Forgive us, Father, for our arrogance. We do not understand how Your mercy and grace work with our Jewish brethren, but the testimony of history demonstrates that You are not finished with them. Judgment belongs only to You. We want to leave it in Your hands, and instead be Your instruments of peace and reconciliation.

Help us, Father. We ask in the Name of Yeshua.

Amen.

"Why Didn't the Christians Help Us?"

by Sharon Sanders

We can read about the atrocities committed against the Jews during the Holocaust (*see entry on The LIST, 1933-45*). We can watch documentaries and movies like Schindler's List to get some kind of an idea of what happened at that time. But there is nothing like personal experience based on real relationships with Holocaust survivors to really get a view into the dark abyss that we call the Holocaust.

It was one of the most uncomfortable moments of my life. I quickly searched for a response to her straightforward question, and the first download that came took me by surprise.

I was in the home of an Auschwitz survivor in Tel Aviv. Mia had invited my German friend and me to visit her. It was the late 1980s and Israelis were hard at work engaged in rebuilding their nation. Very few had time for attending to the emotional and psychological needs of their Holocaust survivors who had made it to their homeland. They were alone. Our knock at their door was music to their ears. Each survivor was attempting to cope with personal memories of the inferno of fire in which they had nearly been reduced to ashes. Still locked behind prison bars of memories, their nightmarish past was still hauntingly etched forever in their outlook on life. Some couldn't recall what they ate for lunch the day before, but every detail of the engravings on Nazi belts and the faces of "Christian" neighbors was committed to memory. Blinded by the lies of Replacement Theology, the negative stereotyping of Jewish people has become an epidemic of antisemitism which still plagues the Church today.

Few had yet divulged their chronicles of the depth of evil to which they had been exposed. A small number of survivors had disclosed their reports of horror to a few. As a result, I was among the earliest Christians to ever enter into the private homes and personal lives of survivors of the holocaust, after their arrival to Israel. These opportunities gave us an advantage over the common understanding of what these people underwent in their traumatic experiences.

We soon began to understand some of the extent of the mental suffering and physical pain each one had endured. On every visit, they would talk about the memories of their lives in the concentration camps, ghettos, and their lonely experiences of tragedy. A number had lost everything except their life. The shoes we put on our feet would be walking where very few Christian feet had ever travelled. These precious people were not free from the camp memories. The conditions they had emerged from had been deplorable and unforgettable. I had yet to learn the extent of the damage that had been done by Christian communities until later.

Pictured above: Sharon Sanders embracing one of the Holocaust survivors.

Mia was reclining on a sofa bed in her Tel Aviv apartment. She was in pain as she told us she had cancer. We had come in unconditional love, reconciliation and pure motives. God had shown me years prior to coming to Israel, that "healing balm" would play an important part of our future. I had not understood the vision, until that day. We soon learned our visits would bring a soothing salve which these people needed for their healing process.

Unexpectedly, Mia looked into my eyes and said, "Sharon, why didn't the Christians help us? They didn't have to love us, but they could have helped us!"

Besides being caught off guard, as her dark eyes penetrated mine, all I knew to say was *"It seems that the Church forgot that Jesus was a Jew!"* She said *"Yes, my friends and I say 'they' (meaning us) don't even know He was Jewish!"* Her question would only be the tip of the iceberg of how the Jewish people felt about Christians in 1985. In contrast to today, those pioneering years were a time when we plowed a lot of fallow ground which needed to be broken up, allowing the seeds of unconditional love to be planted across the country in some 55 cities in Israel.

She had clearly brought with her the nagging reflections of the Jewish community as they considered the attitudes of their "Christian" neighbors during World War II. The Church, all too often, did nothing to prevent mass killing sprees of Jewish people. I believe the Jewish community expected more from Christians than what was shown. It was troublesome for the Jewish communities to accept the arrogant responses flaunted toward their people. The result of Christian indifference, lack of concern and apathy shown had caused Jewish hearts to ache, and yet still they welcomed us into their homes. We found little animosity, nor unforgiveness anywhere we went, but the nagging question mark in Mia's mind cast a giant shadow over the entire Christian world.

Time, hard work and an abundance of unconditional love has poured out a golden era of reconciliation. We shed many a tear, confessed our sin at what Christians had failed to do to help, and told them how sorry we were. We shed tears together. We took this healing balm to countless survivors as we travelled the roads through valleys, plains and deserts of Israel for thirty years. Today, we need much more unconditional love to be shown by the Church around the world.

One survivor, Sima, a survivor of Bergen-Belsen, shared how she had stood in sewer water up to her neck in an outhouse toilet to hide from the Nazis. She refused, at first, to allow me to hug her when we first met. She said *"Your people pulled down the shades, and closed the doors on my people!"* It took two years before she said to me, *"I have watched you with my people, you hug them, you love them, you really do love them. You are not like the people we saw back there (during the Holocaust). You have given me faith in your people again."* She then gave me a big hug which I had waited for, for so long.

We know now that the Christian Church played a big part in the atrocities perpetrated against the Jewish people, sometimes standing by and clapping when Jewish people were shot and thrown into mass graves. How can any Christian stand before God, and any Jewish person, and not ask for forgiveness? How can we say we are a religion of love when "love never fails" (1 Corinthians 13:8)? The Church did fail, and it is time for global repentance coming from churches around the world for the shame brought to the name of Jesus.

Much of the Church is imparting uncertain sounds from our pulpits as it is written in 1 Corinthians 14:8:

> *"For if the trumpet give an uncertain sound, who shall prepare himself to the battle?"* (KJV)

Too many of our shepherds are not interested in bible prophecy being fulfilled, the return of Jesus, and the part which Israel plays in the coming Kingdom. They end up with milque toast sermons, instead of serving meat as it is written in Matthew 24:45:

> *"Who then is a faithful and wise servant, whom his lord hath made ruler over his household, to give them meat in due season?"* (KJV)

Church history and its wicked transgressions against the Jewish people have been buried in the backyards of many of our church cemeteries. Who will prepare our people for the battles ahead, if we do not include Israel, the nation that is a key to world redemption? Christian academia needs to correct its errors of leaving Israel out of our curricula. Our trumpets need to be sounding clear signals about repentance toward the Jewish people in fulfillment of the *"restoration of all things"* (Acts 3:21).

It is time that the universal "Church" humbled herself in regard to the callous and apathetic response to God's Chosen People in the time of their calamity, instead of ignoring a multitude of hideous sins and trying to cover it up and move on. The seducing spirits and doctrines of devils of Replacement Theology are deadly.

Bill Heinrich, author of a study manual on the doctrine of Replacement Theology and Church-sponsored antisemitism, writes in his Introduction:[1]

> *"...the Church has a serious unresolved issue - the confession of sin to the Jewish people and to the LORD, and to ask forgiveness from both."*

Why **didn't we**, the Christians, help them? **"Never Again"** should this question ever have to be asked of us!

Will you pray this repentance prayer with me?

Dear Father God of Israel,

We come in deep shame and sorrow asking for forgiveness of the sins of our Church forefathers and those who have gone before us, paving a distorted view of what a true Christian is. We renounce the sins of breaking the covenant of brotherhood, going against the will of the Father according to Genesis 12:3. We confess and renounce the sins of arrogance and pride, from which we fell into deception. We cut all ties with false theology, the

Replacement of God's Chosen People. There is no biblical basis to back it up. Our prayer of heartfelt repentance is that not even one Jewish person will ever ask again the question, **"Why didn't the Christians help us?"**

Amen.

ENDNOTES:

1. William H. Heinrich, In the Shame of Jesus: The Hidden Story of Church-Sponsored Anti-Semitism, (USA, Evidence of Truth Ministries, Inc., 2008), 11

https://dokumen.tips/download/link/in-the-shame-of-jesus-the-hidden-story-of-church-sponsored-anti-semitism

The Holocaust: The Conspiracies of Silence and Indifference

by Ray Montgomery

"What hurts the victim most is not the cruelty of the oppressor but the silence of the bystander." Elie Wiesel, 2006[1]

"We are at once put to work sorting. My friend Leybl stands next to me. We inspect every garment as carefully as possible. On the other side of me stands a worker who has already been here for several days. I want to find out from him what happened here, since, despite the fact that I can see the clothes left behind by the victims, I still cannot grasp what is going on." Chil Rajchman, author of "The Last Jew of Treblinka"[2]

"Death's Diary: The Parisians

Summer came.
For the book thief, everything was going nicely.
For me, the sky was the color of Jews.

When their bodies had finished scouring for gaps in the door, their souls rose up. When their fingernails had scratched at the wood and in some cases were nailed into it by the sheer force of desperation, their spirits came toward me, into my arms, and we climbed out of those shower facilities, onto the roof and up, into eternity's certain breadth. They just kept feeding me. Minute after minute. Shower after shower." Markus Zusak, author of "The Book Thief"[3]

Six million Jews is the number most often cited as to how many died in the Holocaust in Europe, between 1933 and 1945. But the *total* numbers are far higher.

The United States Holocaust Memorial Museum in Washington DC is the central US repository for the study of the Holocaust (*see entry on The LIST, 1933-45*). Their collection includes photographs, artifacts, films, books, testimonies from Holocaust survivors, and more. In 2000 they began documenting and cataloguing all that data, completing their research in 2013.[4]

This documentation revealed that the Holocaust statistics are far higher than anybody realised. 70 years after the Holocaust, they found that the total number of those who died or were imprisoned was between **15-20 million**. Research also revealed the following:[5]

- Nazi ghettos and camps throughout Europe: 42,500+
- Slave labour camps: 30,000
- Jewish ghettos: 1,150
- Concentration camps: 980
- POW camps: 1,000
- Brothels filled with sex slaves: 500

Pictured above: Barracks at Auschwitz.

Thousands of other camps were used for euthanizing the elderly and infirm, performing forced abortions, Germanising prisoners, or transporting victims to the killing centers. The Warsaw ghetto alone held 500,000 at its height.

Rabbi Benjamin Blech writes:[5]

> *"For years our efforts to understand the Holocaust focused on the perpetrators. We looked for explanations for the madness of Mengele, the obsessive hatred of Hitler, the impassive cruelty of Eichmann. We sought answers to how it was possible for the criminal elements, the sadists and the mentally unbalanced to achieve the kind of power that made the mass killings feasible.*
>
> *That was because we had no idea of the real extent of the horror. With more than 42,000 ghettos and concentration camps scattered throughout the length and breadth of a supposedly civilized continent, there's no longer any way to avoid the obvious conclusion. The cultured, the educated, the enlightened, the liberal, the refined, the sophisticated, the urbane, all of them share in the shame of a world that lost its moral compass and willingly acceded to the victory of evil."*

How is it possible that so many people could live in such denial, when it was impossible for them not to have known what was going on? How is it possible, with the sheer numbers involved as these statistics reveal, for people to have a sort of "collective ignorance"?

Some chose to hide behind denial rather than face the truth. A friend told me that a German woman she knows, who was in Berlin during those days, explained somewhat incredulously *"We just thought they'd all moved away."* Note that she used the collective "we", rather than the more personal "I". Better to spread the blame around, lest it render her personally culpable in some way. Is this how a decent person rationalises things so they can sleep at night? Or was the truth just too terrible to consider? Or was it worse, that she truly didn't care?

Some chose to look the other way, such as Martin Niemöller, the Lutheran pastor who stood by and said nothing - because it wasn't his problem - as memorialised in his poem *"First they came for the socialists, and I did not speak out – because I was not a socialist…"*. But his silence gave tacit approval to what was happening.

Others chose to hide behind the excuse that it was "God's will". After the liberation from the Nazis, author Leon Wells recounts in his book "The Janowska Road"[6] how he tracked down a Polish Catholic woman, to find out why she had led the Gestapo to his mother's hiding place (*see entry on The LIST, 1945*):

"More often we spoke of how our own 'good' non-Jewish neighbors had betrayed us. Why? We didn't expect them to help us, but why did they so enthusiastically help to murder us? I found out where the gentile neighbor who had betrayed my mother now lived, and went there. I was greeted with the familiar, 'I knew that some of you would survive.'

I asked the woman why she had given my mother's hiding place to the SS man after having lived on good terms next door to her for so many years. To this she replied: 'It wasn't Hitler who killed the Jews; it was God's will, and Hitler was his tool. How could I stand by and be against the will of God?'

I walked out, stunned. I hadn't expected that kind of answer. She did not feel that she should repent or even deny her deed."

I find this passage extremely provoking, with the excuse that it was "God's will" still having the power to grieve me deeply. From Haman to Hitler, the Jews have always been singled out for extinction, but the Holocaust was a particularly dark chapter in the world's horrific history of antisemitism.

Perhaps they could no more face the truth than we can. For with the Hitler juggernaut bulldozing its way across Europe, it inevitably begs the question *"What would I have done had it been me standing by watching? What excuse might I have made?"*

Would I be like that woman who consoled her denial with the lame excuse *"We all thought they'd just moved away"?*

Would I say nothing, like Martin Niemöller, because it was somebody else's problem?

Or would I leave it at God's door, hiding behind that good old stand-by trope that it's "God's will", thus absolving me from any personal responsibility?

Perhaps I would have had the courage to actually do something. But what? God forbid that I am ever faced with that decision!

Elie Wiesel, a Holocaust survivor, said in 1986:[1]

"The opposite of love is not hate, it's indifference.
The opposite of art is not ugliness, it's indifference.
The opposite of faith is not heresy, it's indifference.
And the opposite of life is not death, it's indifference.

Because of indifference, one dies before one actually dies. To be in the window and watch people being sent to concentration camps or being attacked in the street and do nothing, that's being dead."

Rabbi Benjamin Blech perhaps sums it up best:[5]

"The unspeakable crime of the 20th Century, more than the triumph of evil, was the sin of the innocent bystander... If we dare to hope for the survival of civilization we had better pray that the pessimists are wrong when they claim that the only thing we learn from history is that mankind never learns from history." (emphasis mine)

The Holocaust was a tragedy that the human race is still trying to come to terms with. But with the global rise of antisemitism reeking eerily of 1938, and the deadliest massacre of Jews to ever occur in the United States resulting in 11 dead in Pittsburgh almost 80 years to the day since *Kristallnacht* (*see entry on The LIST, 2018*), if the past is prologue, perhaps the prescient and piercing question should be, *"What do I do now?"*

"I swore never to be silent whenever and wherever human beings endure suffering and humiliation. We must take sides. Neutrality helps the oppressor, never the victim. Silence encourages the tormentor, never the tormented."
Elie Wiesel[1]

"Thou shalt not be a victim, thou shalt not be a perpetrator, but, above all, thou shalt not be a bystander." Yehuda Bauer[7]

"The question shouldn't be 'Why are you, a Christian, here in a death camp, condemned for trying to save Jews?' The real question is 'Why aren't all the Christians here?'" Joel C. Rosenberg, author of "The Auschwitz Escape"[8]

"And the King will answer them, 'Truly, I say to you, as you did it to one of the least of these my brothers, you did it to me.'" MATTHEW 25:40 (ESV)

Will you pray this repentance prayer with me?

Heavenly Father,

We ask for forgiveness for our role in the Holocaust, for it is something we must face, and own, rather than be guilty of the same excuses our predecessors had, of living in denial, of looking the other way, or of blaming You. Forgive us for what we allowed to happen by being silent, indifferent bystanders to the most horrific antisemitic event in history, the Holocaust. Give us the courage to never be silent again, to do something, no matter what the cost.

In Jesus' name,

Amen.

ENDNOTES:

1. https://en.wikiquote.org/wiki/Elie_Wiesel

2. Chil Rajchman, The Last Jew of Treblinka: A Memoir, (New York, Pegasus Books, 2011), Chapter 3

3. Markus Zusak, The Book Thief, (USA, Random House, 2005), 349

4. https://www.ushmm.org/research

5. http://virtualjerusalem.com/holidays.php?Itemid=25140

6. Leon Weliczker Wells, The Janowska Road, (USA, The Macmillan Company, 1963), 254-255

7. https://en.wikiquote.org/wiki/Yehuda_Bauer

8. Joel C. Rosenberg, The Auschwitz Escape, (USA, Tyndale House Publishers, Inc., 2014), 262

Speaking Out — Part 1

by Ray Montgomery

*"First they came for the communists, and I did not speak out
— because I was not a communist;*

*Then they came for the socialists, and I did not speak out
— because I was not a socialist;*

*Then they came for the trade unionists, and I did not speak out
— because I was not a trade unionist;*

*Then they came for the Jews, and I did not speak out
— because I was not a Jew;*

*Then they came for me
— and there was no one left to speak out for me."*[1]

Martin Niemöller, Lutheran pastor

This famous poem[1] was written about the inactivity of ordinary Germans following the Nazi rise to power, and the purging of their chosen targets, group by group. By failing to speak out while there was still time, Niemöller ended up spending seven years in concentration camps (1938-45).

I personally believe he suffered great remorse for his inaction, this poem being an act of contrition for his silence, silence which had given tacit approval to what the Nazis were doing to various groups of people in Germany in those years. I also believe he redeemed himself in part, for this poem of repentance has been quoted countless times ever since as a cautionary tale against inaction and/or silence.

Pictured above: Martin Niemöller.

But I shudder when I consider how I might feel to stand before the LORD on Judgment Day, if I dare not speak out when the situation necessitates it, in light of this scripture:

> *"And the King will answer them, 'Truly, I say to you, as you did it to one of the least of these my brothers, you did it to me.'"* MATTHEW 25:40 (ESV)

What would we have done in those dark days? Would we have remained silent like Niemöller, using the excuse that it was someone else's problem? Would fear of what might happen if we spoke out have silenced us?

But what if we had dared to speak out against what was happening? Would that have made any difference?

Well, actually, yes. There are two major national examples where thousands of Jews were saved – because a nation of individuals dared to speak up (*for both entries see The LIST, 1943*). On October 1st 1943, Hitler ordered Danish Jews to be arrested and deported. But the Danish resistance movement, with the assistance of many ordinary Danish citizens, managed to evacuate 7,220 of Denmark's 7,800 Jews to Sweden.

Over 99% of Denmark's Jews survived the Holocaust — because people dared to speak up — and do something about it.

Then there was Nazi-allied Bulgaria. Tsar Boris III refused to allow 50,000 Bulgarian Jews to be deported to the concentration camps, thanks to pressure from Bulgarian politicians, the Bulgarian Orthodox Church, and a national public outcry: ordinary citizens and religious leaders threatened to block the path of Holocaust trains by lying on the railroad tracks. Boris III told Hitler he needed the Jews for railroad construction and other industrial work. After the war they emigrated en masse to Israel.

Bulgaria, an Axis power allied with Nazi-Germany, defied Hitler's demands — and saved all its Jews — because people spoke out!

What would have happened had Martin Niemöller dared to speak out? Would others have rallied and supported him? Would the course of the war have been changed and millions of lives be saved? We'll never know, but his poem contains a truth generally attributed to Edmund Burke, an Irish born Member of Parliament in the House of Commons from 1766-94:

"All that is necessary for the triumph of evil is that good men do nothing."[2]

But would we speak out, even if we knew it wouldn't change anything? Augustine Pozdech, a Catholic priest in Slovakia, sent the following letter in April 1942 to the Jewish community of Budapest, Hungary, rather than the Vatican, asking them to intervene for the Jews of Slovakia (*see entry on The LIST, April 1942*):

"You may find it strange that a Catholic priest addressed you about this subject. I decided upon this action because it is impossible for me to remain a silent witness of the horrible sufferings that afflicts my Jewish neighbours. I am appalled to the bottom of my heart as human beings, who have no fault other than being born Jews, have their property stolen from them, forced onto trains with the remnant of their personal freedom, and sent to a foreign country as slaves.

I wish to awaken the conscience of the world against this persecution. But alas, I am not able to make my words heard beyond this narrow circle. It is you, to whom I urge, to wake up and shake the conscience of the world, so that the atrocious suffering of the Jews in Slovakia be relieved. However, it is impossible that the world witnesses this and remains inactive, while little children, the mortally ill elderly, young girls torn from their families and young people are deported like cattle: transports of livestock wagons going to an unknown place, to an uncertain future.

Act, before it is too late, act quickly, and it may still be possible to save some of Slovakian Jewry.

I hope my words will be heard, I hope you will do everything possible for the sake of your poor, unfortunate coreligionists."

There is no indication he received a reply, but at least he tried. And more importantly: heaven, a cloud of witnesses, and the LORD Himself — noticed!

So when do we start speaking out? One of the lessons I have learned from The LIST is that it is not enough just to repent of the sins of our Church forefathers.

We need to do more than that: we need to speak out against antisemitism in particular — and injustice in general — wherever and whenever we find it. Whenever I hear an antisemitic comment — I nip it in the bud. Whenever I hear a skewed statement that reflects an anti-Israel bias — either because of something repeated from the news, or simply a lack of knowledge about Israel's history, or whatever — I comment accordingly, and hopefully educate in the process. And the more I do this, the easier it gets, for it is becoming second nature now to do so.

The time to do this is now, while it is still easy to speak out. For the day may come, God forbid, when it is too late to speak out, as Martin Niemöller found to his cost.

> *"If I am not for myself, then who will be for me? And if I am only for myself, then what am I? And if not now, when?"* Hillel the Elder[3], one of the most important religious figures in Jewish history.

For if we don't speak up now, while we still can, we run the risk of fulfilling George Santayana's maxim:[4]

> *"Those who fail to learn from the mistakes of their predecessors are destined to repeat them."*

Our silence, in not speaking out against antisemitism, would be tacit approval of it. For if we fail to speak out in defense of our Jewish brethren, and on their behalf, standing shoulder to shoulder with them, we risk hearing these chilling words from the LORD on that day, with its eternal implications:

> *"And the King will answer them, 'Truly, I say to you, as you did it to one of the least of these my brothers, you did it to me.'"* MATTHEW 25:40

I'm sure everyone is familiar with the proverb "For Want of a Nail":

> *"For want of a nail the shoe was lost.*
> *For want of a shoe the horse was lost.*
> *For want of a horse the rider was lost.*
> *For want of a rider the message was lost.*
> **For want of a message** *the battle was lost.*
> *For want of a battle the kingdom was lost.*
> *And all for the want of a nail."*

All it takes is for one voice to speak out with a message. And if that one voice is joined by others all saying the same message, leading to a nation of people all speaking out — like the Danes and Bulgarians did — perhaps six million Jews wouldn't have been lost. It begins with that "voice of one crying out in the wilderness." Are we that voice? Will our voices form a united chorus, with a united message? Will that message change the course of history?

"...it is appointed for man to die once, and after that comes judgment"
HEBREWS 9:27 (ESV)

Will you pray this repentance prayer with me?

Heavenly Father,

We thank You for Martin Niemöller's contrition, as reflected in his poem, and we pray what we might learn the lesson he failed to learn in time: to speak out. We ask that You give us the courage to make our voices heard, wherever and whenever injustice and antisemitism arises, and to speak words of grace and truth in a spirit of love.

Having learnt the lessons listed above, we resolve to start doing this now, so that it not only becomes second nature, but collectively we can become a chorus of voices all speaking out the same message. Let us not lose any more lives, nor let our silence be a cause for the repetition of history.

Strengthen us for this task. Bring assistance along the way. Bind our hearts to those of like minds. Glorify Your name through our speaking out.

In Jesus' name,

Amen.

ENDNOTES:

1. https://en.wikiquote.org/wiki/Martin_Niem%C3%B6ller
   https://en.wikipedia.org/wiki/First_they_came_...

2. https://en.wikiquote.org/wiki/Edmund_Burke

3. https://en.wikipedia.org/wiki/Hillel_the_Elder

4. https://en.wikiquote.org/wiki/George_Santayana

Speaking Out — Part 2

by Ray Montgomery

"If I were to remain silent, I'd be guilty of complicity." Albert Einstein[1]

Most of our LIST has focused on the negative developments of Replacement Theology over the centuries, and persecution of Jews by Christians. But there have been those who have spoken out and acted to help Jews. And of the many examples that could be quoted, there are two truly inspiring stories worth mentioning in detail.

Roddie Edmonds (1919-1985)

(see entry on The LIST, January 1945)

The first story concerns Master Sgt. Roddie Edmonds, a Christian, who was captured in the Battle of the Bulge in late 1944. He spent 100 days in captivity, first at the POW camp Stalag IX-B before being transferred in January 1945, along with other enlisted personnel, to camp Stalag IX-A (near Ziegenhain, Germany), where he was the senior ranking US non-commissioned officer. The Nazis had a strict policy of separating Jews from non-Jews. By then most of the infamous Nazi death camps were no longer fully operational, so any Jewish-American POWs were instead sent to slave labour camps, where their chances of survival would have been low.

On the first day of his captivity the camp Commandant ordered Edmonds to tell *only the Jewish-American soldiers* to present themselves at the next morning's assembly. Knowing this would mean certain death for the Jewish prisoners, he ordered all 1,275 men to present themselves.

Pictured above: Roddie Edmonds and the American soldiers who lined up in front of the barracks at Ziegenhain.

Paul Stern, a Jewish POW saved by Edmonds, said in his testimony to Yad Vashem "Although seventy years have passed, I can still hear the words he said to the German camp commander." Here's how he described it:[2]

> *"After a number of days at Ziegenhain, the German commander ordered all Jewish American POW's to line up the* [sic] *in front of the barracks the following morning. At that point, Master Sergeant Roddie Edmonds informed all American soldiers to line up in military formation in front of the barracks the following morning. When the German commander saw the large contingent of POW's, he said to Sergeant Edmonds "You all can't be Jews", whereupon Sergeant Edmonds replied, "We are all Jews here." At that point the German commander put his gun against Edmonds forehead and said, "You will order all Jews to step forward, or I will shoot you right now." As I recall, Sergeant Edmonds then said, "The Geneva Convention states that if a soldier is captured he need only provide his name, rank and serial number. If you shoot me, you will have to shoot all of us, because we all know who you are, and when the war is over you will be tried as a war criminal." At that point, the German commander left, and we all returned to our barracks. With that one act of courage, Sergeant Edmonds saved my life, as well as all the Jewish prisoners at Ziegenhain."* Paul Stern

Shortly thereafter the camp was liberated by General Patton. Edmond's actions saved about 200 Jews.

His heroism would have remained unknown when he died in 1985, were it not for the diaries he had kept, and which his son, Baptist Rev. Chris Edmonds, started reading. These diaries not only included some of his daily thoughts, but also the names and addresses of his men. Later, with the internet, Chris was able to unravel what we now know. Chris said he believed his father had a "deep moral conviction" instilled in his faith that inspired his actions. *"All he had to fight with was his will power and his wits,"* he said. *"I'm just glad he did the right thing."*[3]

On February 10th, 2015, Yad Vashem recognised him as Righteous Among the Nations, the first American serviceman to receive the honour, which was presented to his son, Chris. He is also being considered for a Congressional Medal of Honour, America's highest and most prestigious personal military decoration.[4]

Nicholas Winton (1909-2015)

The second inspiring story concerns Nicholas Winton, a British humanitarian who organised the rescue of 669 children, mostly Jewish, from Czechoslovakia on the eve of World War II, in an operation later known as the Czech *Kindertransport* or "children's transport" (*see entry on The LIST, 2015*). He found homes for them and arranged their safe passage to Britain, but it wouldn't be until 1988 that the world found out what he'd done, following his wife's discovery of a scrapbook in the attic, which happened to include a list of all the children he had saved.

In 1938, violence against Jews was increasing in Germany. The 1938 Munich Agreement paved the way for Hitler's armies to march unopposed into the German speaking area of Czechoslovakia, the Sudetenland, on October 1st. Prague was filled with refugees desperate to escape, so Winton visited Czechoslovakia to see if there was anything he could do to help. The people he met knew that war was coming, and while they themselves couldn't get out, they were desperate to save their children. Operating under his guiding principle:

> *"Anything that is not actually impossible can be done, if one really sets one's mind to do it and is determined that it shall be done."*[5] Nicholas Winton

Winton set up shop in a hotel in Prague, and created an organisation with the aim of getting as many children out as possible.

When he returned to London he took stationery from an established refugee organisation, the "British Committee for Refugees from Czechoslovakia", added the words "Children's Section" beneath, made himself Chairman, put his mother in charge, recruited a staff of volunteers, and started dealing with the British bureaucracy. (Yes, fraud!) The British authorities agreed to accept the children, but only if families were willing to take them in, so he circulated the children's photos to "advertise" them. As the authorities were slow in issuing travel documents, he resorted to using money (yes, blackmail!) to have them forged to speed up the process. (Yes, forgery!)

When asked if he asked anyone else to help, he said he approached America, but *"The Americans wouldn't take any, which was a pity. We could have got a lot more out."*

The first 20 children left Prague on March 14th, 1939. The next day German troops marched into Prague and the rest of Czechoslovakia. Over the spring and summer of 1939, the Nazis allowed seven trains to leave, in keeping with their policy of cleansing Europe of its Jews. An eighth train with 250 children aboard was scheduled to leave on September 1st, but that was the day war was declared. It is doubtful any of those children survived, as two years later the Nazis began implementing the Final Solution. Czech Jews were sent to Theresienstadt, a hybrid concentration camp/ghetto in Terezin, about 40 miles north of Prague. From there it was a one-way journey to Auschwitz...

In 1988 his story came out when the BBC featured him in an episode of "That's Life".[6] Surrounding him in the audience, and asked to stand, were more than two-dozen of the children he'd saved, now fully grown adults. In an interview on 60 Minutes[7], he said that this was the most emotional moment of his life. In short, his 2-week vacation ended up with 669 children, and 15,000 grandchildren and great-grandchildren. *"It's a terrible responsibility, isn't it?"* he joked.

Pictured above: Nicholas Winton with one of the Czech Jewish children he rescued, January 11th, 1939. Video of this evacuation is available on wikipedia.[8]

In 1983 he received an MBE (Member of the Order of the British Empire) for his work in establishing the Abbeyfield homes for the elderly in Britain.[8] In 2003 he was knighted by the Queen for *"services to humanity, in saving Jewish children from Nazi Germany occupied Czechoslovakia"*. The British press dubbed him the "British Schindler." In 2014 he was awarded the highest honour of the Czech Republic, the Order of the White Lion (1st class) by Czech President Miloš Zeman. The minor planet "19384 Winton" was named in his honour by Czech astronomers Jana Tichá and Miloš Tichý. He was awarded the Freedom of the City of London on February 23rd 2015.

Baptised and raised as a Christian by his parents, his Jewish ancestry disqualified him from being declared "Righteous Among the Nations" in Israel. Not that it mattered to him. As far as he was concerned, his actions weren't anything extraordinary.

Summary

I find these stories to be particularly inspiring, both for their heroism in the way they chose to speak out (and act accordingly), and for their respective humility. Neither of them broadcast what they had done, their stories subsequently being uncovered by accident.

But rest assured that heaven, a cloud of witnesses, and the LORD Himself — noticed!

Will you pray this prayer of praise and thanksgiving with me?

Heavenly Father,

We thank You that there have been those Christians in history who have spoken out on behalf of Your chosen people. Let us be encouraged, and inspired, by their example, to speak out likewise.

And we thank You for Roddie Edmonds and Nicholas Winton in particular, whose stories are truly inspiring, and whose legacies can be found in the Jews who survived, and their descendants. We ask that their examples, of speaking out, will serve as an inspiration to us to do the same, to stand by Your chosen people, shoulder to shoulder, in these days.

In Jesus' precious name,

Amen.

ENDNOTES:

1. https://www.goodreads.com/quotes/4466-if-i-were-to-remain-silent-i-d-be-guilty-of

2. https://www.yadvashem.org/righteous/stories/edmonds/paul-stern-testimony.html

3. https://www.independent.co.uk/news/world/americas/sgt-roddie-edmonds-us-veteran-who-risked-his-life-by-refusing-to-hand-jews-to-nazis-posthumously-a6757506.html

4. https://en.wikipedia.org/wiki/Roddie_Edmonds

5. http://goodyawards.com/8-inspirational-quotes-by-humble-hero-sir-nicholas-winton/

6. https://www.youtube.com/watch?v=PKkgO06bAZk

7. https://www.youtube.com/watch?v=c0aoifNziKQ&t=341s

8. https://en.wikipedia.org/wiki/Nicholas_Winton

The Voyages of The Exodus 1947 and the MS St. Louis

by Laura Densmore

Pictured above: The Exodus 1947.

Exodus 1947

Two years after the end of World War II, on July 11, 1947, the ship, Exodus 1947, set sail from the port of Sète on the Mediterranean shores of France[1] (*see entry on The LIST, 1947*). On board were 4,515 Jewish Holocaust survivors, 1,672 of them being children and teens.[2] These Jewish survivors had come from all over Europe, leaving everything behind, carrying all their worldly belongings in a suitcase. They were leaving the horrors of the Holocaust behind them. Before them lay Palestine, the Promised Land of hope, freedom, and new beginnings. The only problem was that Palestine was still under British control. The British Mandate for Palestine was a League of Nations mandate that came into effect in 1923, with the United Kingdom as the administering authority, to establish the 1917 Balfour Declaration's "national home for the Jewish people", and Transjordan.[3]

Other ships had attempted to bring Jewish immigrants to Palestine and had failed. This was a long shot. But, with hopes, tears, determination and grit, the Jewish American crew of 35 volunteers set off into Mediterranean waters bound for Bat Yam, a port just south of Tel Aviv.

Why were the British so focused on preventing Jews from returning to their ancient homeland? Why would they send destroyers after a ship carrying unarmed Jewish Holocaust survivors whose only wish was to find a place where they could live in peace?

Following the pattern of earlier British White Papers[4], the White Paper of 1939 severely restricted Jewish immigration to Palestine. Understandably, the British were trying to walk a tightrope of balance. They depended on Arab oil exports and felt they must not anger their Arab partners by allowing too many Jews into the region. The British were caught in the middle of a Jewish-Arab conflict.

The passengers on board had just enough food, water and provisions for two weeks, which was more than enough for the voyage. The ship had originally been outfitted to carry 500 passengers. When it was retrofitted for this voyage, enough bunks were built to carry the 4,515 passengers. Time was of the essence. They needed to reach their destination before running out of food and water.

During the entire voyage, the ship was followed by British destroyers. Finally, as they approached the more southern Egyptian shore waters, the ship made a sudden turn northward to head for the Bat Yam port in Israel.

The British navy had no intention of allowing the Exodus reach the shores of Israel. In the dark of night, the Exodus 1947 was hemmed in on both sides by two British destroyers. The ship was being squeezed from both sides. The British blared over the loudspeakers:

> *"You are in territorial waters. You are under arrest. Stop your ship."*

The Exodus 1947 continued steaming ahead.

The British then forcibly rammed the ship and began boarding the Exodus 1947, bringing guns and tear gas. The Jewish refugees fought back with tins of beef and potatoes.

After being forcibly rammed by the British destroyers, the vessel was no longer seaworthy, and the passengers were forced to disembark. The conflict left 146 people injured and three people dead.

The once hopeful immigrants were then forced onto three British prison ships, which returned them to the shores of France. When the ships arrived on August 2nd at Port-de-Bouc, the French Government told the passengers they could disembark on a voluntary basis. None of the refugees did. The Jews were making their stand!

By this time the world media had picked up the story. Stories and pictures of the Jewish refugees trapped on board the prison ships were being sent all over the world in newsreels and the press. And while they sat in stifling, hot and cramped quarters on board the prison ships, the UN committee was meeting to decide what to do with the "Palestine problem".

The Foreign Secretary of England, Ernest Bevin, gave the Jews on board the ships an ultimatum: get off the ships within 24 hours or be shipped back to Germany! Only twenty-one refugees got off.

Incredibly, the British then sent the three prison ships back to Germany, to the nation that had murdered 6 million Jews in the Holocaust.

The ships arrived at the Hamburg Germany port in August 1947, after which the Jewish refugees staged a sit-down strike. The Holocaust survivors were then clubbed, tear-gassed, fire-hosed, and forcibly taken off the ships and sent to detention camps. In one case a Jew *"was dragged down the gangway by the feet with his head bumping on the wooden slats"*.[1]

The media covered the terrible treatment of the Jews and denounced Great Britain. World leaders in the United Nations called for an end to British control of Palestine.

This highly publicized incident heavily influenced the decision that would ultimately be made at the United Nations to partition Palestine into an Arab and a Jewish state. This black mark in history was actually turned around by God for His purposes for Israel.

Just three months later, on November 29th, 1947, the United Nations voted and approved UN Resolution 181 which ended British control of Palestine, created the blueprint for a two-state solution, and paved the way for the creation of the Jewish state of Israel. The Exodus 1947 voyage acted as a catalyst in forming the new State of Israel.

While Britain was highly culpable in the shameful incident of the Exodus, those of us who reside in other countries must understand that Britain was not the only nation that failed to support the Jews in making their way to a safe haven, as the following story illustrates.

MS St. Louis

The MS St. Louis, a luxury cruise liner, left Hamburg, Germany on May 13th, 1939 (*see entry on The LIST, 1939*). This was four months before the onset of World War II. Led by their captain, Gustav Schröder, 937 German Jews were bound for Cuba in hopes of escaping the Nazi regime. Most had sold all their belongings to book their passage, pay off corrupt German officials, and buy visas to Cuba. As the ship came into the Havana port, hope turned to despair when port officials suddenly barred their entry. For thirty excruciating days, the St. Louis wandered the seas and was refused haven by Cuba, Canada and the United States.

The United States Holocaust Memorial Museum notes:[5]

> *"Sailing so close to Florida that they could see the lights of Miami, some passengers on the St. Louis cabled President Franklin D. Roosevelt asking for refuge. Roosevelt never responded."*

The movie, Voyage of the Damned,[6] tells the story of the MS St. Louis. There is one scene in the movie where the Gestapo agent from Havana is having a conversation with the captain of the ship. He says these chilling words:

> *"It was never intended for your passengers to land. But can't you see? We force the world to realize that there is a problem with these people, the Jews. So when we rid Germany of the problem, no one will have the right to object."*

The captain sailed the ship back to Antwerp, Belgium where the refugees were finally accepted by Holland, France, Belgium, and England.

Just four months later, World War II broke out. Many Jews from the MS St. Louis were later caught in Nazi roundups of Jews in occupied countries. By the end of the Holocaust, 254 of them would perish.[7]

Will you pray this repentance prayer with me?

Heavenly Father,

We all stand in horror, and our hearts are broken. How can this be? The UK prevented Jews from making it to their homeland after World War II. Canada, Cuba and the United States failed to receive the Jews who were fleeing for their lives just prior to the start of World War II.

Abba, I am so ashamed that my own country of birth turned the Jews away when they most needed our help. Abba, those of us in France, Britain, Germany, Canada, the United States and Cuba ask for Your forgiveness for these decisions that were made.

Abba, we see that this is an issue of the heart. When our own hearts are cold, callous and selfish, even we could perpetrate such crimes against innocent ones.

Abba, please break up the fallow ground in our hearts. Please go deep to find any stony places. Expose and reveal the mindsets and beliefs in us that would allow us to behave in a cold, calculating or cruel manner towards our Jewish brethren. Abba, please do a "heart transplant" in us: take out the heart of stone and put in a heart of flesh so that we will love our fellow man, and love our Jewish brothers and sisters - not just in words, but in deeds.

In Yeshua's name,

Amen.

> *"I will give you a new heart and put a new spirit within you; I will take the heart of stone out of your flesh and give you a heart of flesh. I will put My Spirit within you and cause you to walk in My statutes, and you will keep My judgments and do them."* EZEKIEL 36:26-27 (NKJV)

ENDNOTES:

1. https://en.wikipedia.org/wiki/SS_Exodus

2. For more details about the Exodus 1947 voyage, watch the award winning documentary at: https://www.exodus1947.com/

3. https://en.wikipedia.org/wiki/British_Mandate_for_Palestine_(legal_instrument)

4. https://www.jewishvirtuallibrary.org/the-british-white-papers

5. https://www.ushmm.org/educators/teaching-materials/national-history-day/research-topics/the-st.-louis

6. For more details about the MS St. Louis voyage, watch the movie, "Village of the Damned", available on Amazon prime videos.

7. https://en.wikipedia.org/wiki/MS_St._Louis

The Miracle of Israel's Resurrection!

by Christine Darg

From the list of atrocities against the Jews, we see, tragically, that churches have not understood that the God of Israel is a faithful covenant-keeper! More than ever, the Church must comprehend the unique time, according to Psalm 102:13, where it is written:

"You will arise and have mercy on Zion;
For the time to favor her,
Yes, the set time, has come." (NKJV)

We are privileged to live now — because the set time when God favors Zion and the restoration of Israel has come!

Thankfully during the Reformation, much biblical ground was recovered, such as the doctrine of *sola scriptura* — the complete reliance on Scripture — as well as sola fide, the belief that faith in Jesus is the way to obtain God's pardon for sin. However, as The LIST documents, the most prominent leader in the Protestant Reformation, Martin Luther, also woefully engaged in virulent antisemitism toward the end of his life. His antisemitic writings against the Jews became the ammunition the Nazis needed to legitimize their persecution of the Jews during the Nazi Holocaust (*see entries in The LIST: 1538, 1543*).

Exploits Ministry took a prayer team to parts of Europe where the Protestant Reformation flourished. Our mission was to believe God for an ongoing Reformation for the Church to rid itself of the error of Replacement Theology, known as supersessionism. Replacement Theology maintains that the Church has succeeded the Israelites as the definitive people of God.

But what does the bible teach? The New Testament teaches that God is not finished with the Jewish people, and that in the Last Days, all of Israel will be saved and be grafted back into the olive tree of God when the fullness of the Gentiles has been received into the Church. That is the teaching of Romans 9, 10 and 11 and other scriptures. We are presently living in a unique period of grace that is overlapping the Church Age and the rising again of Israel. What a glorious time to be watchmen on the walls!

The prophecy of Simeon in Luke 2 is coming to pass before our eyes. The Holy Spirit had revealed to him that he would not die before seeing the LORD's Messiah. Simeon was in the Temple when Mary and Joseph presented the baby Jesus as required by Torah. Simeon took the baby in his arms and praised God, prophesying that Jesus was:

> *"a light for revelation to the Gentiles, and the glory of your people Israel."*
> LUKE 2:32 (NIV)

In a few short words, he prophesied the history of Israel up to the present time. He went on to say:

> *"...This child is set for the **fall** and **rising again** of many in Israel; and for a sign which shall be spoken against... that the thoughts of many hearts will be revealed." Luke 2:34-35* (AMERICAN KJV, emphasis mine)

Simeon warned Mary that the child Immanuel was to be a sign, but the sign would not win acceptance. The destiny of Jesus was to endure the contradiction of sinners, to be a rock of offence. No doubt Simeon had in mind Isaiah 8:14-15:

> *"He shall become a sanctuary; but. . . a rock to stumble over. . ."* (NASB)

Yet Simeon also foresaw that the Jewish people would rise again! In Romans 11:11, Paul asks:

> *"...Did they [Jewish people] stumble so as to fall beyond recovery? Not at all! Rather, because of their transgression, salvation has come to the Gentiles..."* (NIV)

Amen! My friend Bob O'Dell, co-founder of Root Source, pointed out that "rising again" in Luke 2:34 is *anastasis*, which literally means resurrection! Simeon literally said, "This holy one is set for the fall and resurrection of many in Israel!"

Dear friends, we're watching the resurrection of Israel! (*see entry in The LIST, 1948*). If only the Church could fully comprehend this! Sadly, the Church is missing it! Key prophetic events related to the resurrected state of Israel have already happened! The Church must recognize and not oppose this wonderful phenomenon!

Why isn't the universal Church celebrating reborn Israel's milestones and rejoicing in the faithfulness of God? Many of these milestones — 40 years of peace with Egypt, 50 years of a united Jerusalem, 70 years of statehood, 120 years since the first Zionist Congress — are considered by theologians to be the lifespan of a generation (*see entries in The LIST: 1897, 1967, 1948*). It's a new day and a new chapter for the Jewish people! I believe Israel and the remnant Church will come together as the People of the Book.

In Honor of Israel's 70th Birthday!

Pictured above: Remembering Israel's 70th birthday, 2018.

Today the Bible is coming alive in the City of David; stunning archeological discoveries are continually being uncovered. While we cannot condone all the policies of a secular Jewish state, we must recognize that many bible prophecies are being fulfilled about the restoration of the Jewish people to their homeland. Any church that fights against Israel's existence is fighting the God of Israel Himself.

Because Israel is still a secular state and allows abortions and other anti-biblical practices, many in the Church self-righteously point fingers at Israel and claim that God could not possibly be associated with the state of Israel. Today's justice-oriented younger generation see Palestinian Arabs as victims; yet short-sighted Christians who despise Zionism don't comprehend that God said he would bring the Jewish people back to their own land before their spiritual revival. Only after the Jewish people are resettled in their own land will they experience revival. Prophecy in scripture is clear that a time of cleansing, repentance and revival for Israel comes after the Ezekiel 38 and 39 war and after the Holy Spirit outpouring described in Zechariah 12 and 13. Watchmen on the walls must get behind what God is doing and make sure that we are involved in churches and organizations that understand the times and biblical prophecy.

Entire denominations have engaged in the Boycott, Divest, Sanction (BDS) movement which harms Israel economically (*see entry in The LIST, 2005*). Shocking antisemitism has re-emerged which is driving the Jewish people home to Israel! How did the churches and universities succumb to such error?

Many pastors cater to the younger generation and fail to teach their congregations to avoid the "gloom and doom" of eschatology and the study of the End Times. They refuse to teach Bible prophecy, End Times and Israel because one pastor said: "they don't study it or understand it". The second, and perhaps the real reason is this: shamefully they fear scaring people away and losing offerings.

On top of it all, the so-called emergent Church wants to yoke with Rome rather than with God's eternal city, Jerusalem.

Meanwhile, Israel is a miracle of preservation. Jeremiah 31:10 is a living word today:

> *"Hear the word of the Lord, you nations; proclaim it in distant coastlands: 'He who scattered Israel will gather them and keep them and will watch over his flock like a shepherd.'"* (NIV)

After the Holocaust, only God can be protecting the beleaguered Jews in such a dangerous Mideast neighbourhood! All churches must acknowledge the greatness of God and the miracle he has wrought for the Jewish people in the face of unspeakable hostilities.

While Israel is on the verge of receiving the outpouring of the Holy Spirit and the greatest end-time revival, it's no coincidence that the fullness of the Gentiles is materializing in the Church. More Muslims have come to a saving knowledge of Jesus in the last 25 years than in the entire history of Christian missions to Islam.[1,2] The move of the Holy Spirit throughout the Islamic world is one of the signs that Jesus is coming soon and that the times of the Gentiles are winding up.

While apostasy is growing in western churches, it's a different story in Africa, Asia and oppressive regimes such as Iran. The Mohabat Iranian Christian News Agency reported that *"Christianity has been growing at an exponential rate in the last couple of decades in Iran, causing the Islamic government a great deal of concern."*[3] In China, it's estimated there are more disciples of Jesus than members of the Communist Party![4]

Our ministry has experienced tremendous spiritual warfare in the great nation of India because the powers of darkness are running scared of Christianity. It's estimated that across the globe, followers of Jesus are increasing by tens of thousands of souls every day. We often cry *"Maranatha,* Jesus come quickly," yet every day that His return is delayed, the Lord's Bride becomes a full-figured bride—more Gentiles are saved!

I watch Zechariah 8:19, a verse that prophesies that the mourning days and the fast days of Israel will be transformed:

> *"...The fasts of the fourth, fifth, seventh and tenth months will become joyful and glad occasions and happy festivals for Judah..."* (NIV)

I feel led of the Holy Spirit every year to be in Israel on the 9th of Av to pray and to observe that day of mourning (over the destruction of the two Temples). I believe one day this day of mourning will morph into a day of powerful rejoicing!

Will you pray this repentance prayer with me?

> Heavenly Father, we do humble ourselves and repent on behalf of past and present atrocities of the blind and unbelieving Church. Empower the remnant Church to be watchmen on the walls. We do believe that You are restoring Israel at this time. Therefore, we pray into the words of Psalm 106:4-5:

> *"Remember us when you show favor to your people, come to our aid when you save them, that we may enjoy the prosperity of your chosen ones, that we may share in the joy of your nation and join your inheritance in giving praise."* (NIV, paraphrase mine)

> In Yeshua's Name we pray,

> Amen and Amen!

ENDNOTES:

1. https://world.wng.org/2014/07/the_rising_tide_of_muslim_converts_to_christianity

2. http://www.ncregister.com/daily-news/why-are-millions-of-muslims-becoming-christian

3. http://mohabatnews.com/en/?p=3660

4. https://www.theguardian.com/commentisfree/2015/jul/30/china-christianity-removal-crosses-communist-party-churches

Demonising the "Other" — Words *Still* Matter Today

by Ray Montgomery

"The tongue also is a fire, a world of evil among the parts of the body. It corrupts the whole body, sets the whole course of one's life on fire, and is itself set on fire by hell." JAMES 3:6 (NIV)

"The tongue has the power of life and death..." PROVERBS 18:21 (NIV)

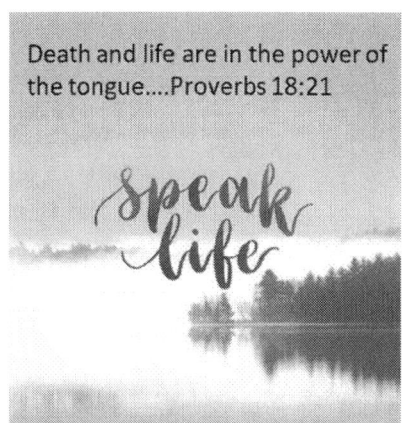

Pictured above: Speak Life.

Consider the following representative sample from each millennium of the words our Church forefathers have said about our Jewish brethren (*see entries on The LIST for the respective years*).

From the 4th Century:

"A synagogue is a brothel and theater, and a cave of pirates and the lair of wild beasts, and the Jews behave no better than hogs and goats in their lewd grossness and the excesses of the gluttony." St. John Chrysostom, Archbishop of Constantinople, Church father, 386-87

From the 16th Century:

> *"The Jews are full of the devil's feces, which they wallow in like swine."*
> Martin Luther, German priest who sparked the Reformation, monk, professor of theology, 1543

Is it any wonder that with words like these, Jewish history for the past two millennia has been saturated with persecutions, murder, expulsions, pogroms, Crusades, Auto-da-fés, Inquisitions, (not to mention a Holocaust!), all perpetrated by Christians and Christian nations – as summarised in The LIST?

> *"They [Christians] sow the wind and [Jews] reap the whirlwind..."*
> HOSEA 8:7 (NIV, paraphrase mine)

But lest we be tempted to think that this is all historical, and things like this aren't said anymore, consider the words of the president of American Vision, "a Biblical Worldview Ministry", who wrote an article in 2010 called "Jerusalem, Mother of Harlots"[1] (*see entry on The LIST, 2010*). In it he claims that Jerusalem is the mystery whore Babylon, and that because Jesus is the *"Final Sacrifice, the sacrifices at the Temple became idolatrous and pagan... Within a generation, the idolatrous, adulterous nation – the great whore Temple in Jerusalem – suffered a final blow from God. It was destroyed into oblivion."*

He concludes:

> *"The Old Jewish people were not merely exiled from their kingdom someday to return. No. This time, the kingdom was taken from them and given to the true nation. Christ created a new bride. Why would Christ desire to return to the whore he has cast aside and divorced when He has a pristine Bride descending from heaven, uncorrupted by idolatry? He didn't. He left that whore riding her patron, the beast of Rome. And the great mother of harlots suffered the judgment of her whoredom. She was divorced and disinherited. The inheritance now belongs to the Bride."*

Does any of this vitriol sound familiar? It should, for our Church forefathers have been uttering words like these for the past 2,000 years. Words like these, uttered in the 21st Century, cut me to the quick, and leave me feeling dumbfounded, sickened, disgusted, and deeply wounded. So how must it make the LORD feel?

It all began when we lost sight of Jews' *humanity*. Once we did that, it became easy to demonise them as the "other". And once they were demonised, it was easy to hate them. And once they were hated, it was easy to kill them. But the process began with the words we spoke, which came from within our own hearts:

> *"A good man brings good things out of the good stored up in his heart, and an evil man brings evil things out of the evil stored up in his heart. For the mouth speaks what the heart is full of."* LUKE 6:45 (NIV)

*"But the things that come out of a person's mouth come from the heart, **and these defile them.**"* MATTHEW 15:18 (NIV, emphasis mine)

We should remember that Creation came into being by Divine Fiat as outlined in Genesis 1 (NIV, emphases mine):

³ *And God SAID, "Let there be light."*

⁶ *And God SAID, "Let there be a vault between the waters to separate water from water."*

⁹ *And God SAID, "Let the water under the sky be gathered to one place…"*

¹¹ *Then God SAID, "Let the land produce vegetation…"*

¹⁴ *And God SAID, "Let there be lights in the vault of the sky…"*

²⁰ *And God SAID, "Let the water teem with living creatures…"*

²⁴ *And God SAID, "Let the land produce living creatures according to their kinds…"*

²⁶ ***Then God SAID, "Let us make mankind in our image…"***

We are created in the image of God, and so our words have creative power – like His. Satan cannot create, but he CAN harness the words we say, and use them to wreak his damage in our lives and in the lives of those around us.

"Kind words bring life, but cruel words crush your spirit." PROVERBS 15:4 (GNT)

"Rumors are dainty morsels that sink deep into one's heart." PROVERBS 18:8 (NLT)

"The human spirit can endure in sickness, but a crushed spirit who can bear?" PROVERBS 18:14 (NIV)

Our words have creative power – for good, or for evil. And then, hypocritically, we go to church on Sunday and sing praises to the LORD, as presumably our Church forefathers cited above did:

"With the tongue we praise our Lord and Father, and with it we curse human beings, who have been made in God's likeness. Out of the same mouth come praise and cursing. My brothers and sisters, this should not be."
JAMES 3:9-10 (NIV)

"Those who consider themselves religious and yet do not keep a tight rein on their tongues deceive themselves, and their religion is worthless." JAMES 1:26 (NIV)

Let us learn from our repugnant history of what damning speech can lead to, and set a guard over our mouths, so that the words we speak create life, healing and encouragement:

"Do not let any unwholesome talk come out of your mouths, but only what is helpful for building others up according to their needs, that it may benefit those who listen." EPHESIANS 4:29 (NIV)

"Let your conversation be always full of grace..." COLOSSIANS 4:6 (NIV)

"The words of the reckless pierce like swords, but the tongue of the wise brings healing." PROVERBS 12:18 (NIV)

If we don't heed the lessons from history, about what the spoken word led to with regard to our Jewish brethren, we do so at our peril, with these eternal consequences:

"For by your words you will be justified, and by your words you will be condemned." MATTHEW 12:37 (ESV)

"Those who guard their lips preserve their lives, but those who speak rashly will come to ruin." PROVERBS 13:3 (NIV)

"Those who guard their mouths and their tongues keep themselves from calamity." PROVERBS 21:23 (NIV)

"I tell you that on the day of judgment people will have to account for every careless word they speak." MATTHEW 12:36 (CSB)

Will you pray this repentance prayer with me?

Heavenly Father,

We have read the negative words our Church forefathers uttered, and seen the consequences of that destructive power unleashed, and we ask for forgiveness. We also ask for forgiveness for the words our Church forefathers uttered, using Your Holy Scriptures to justify their own bigotry against Your chosen people, and we ask for forgiveness. We ask that You do a deep work within our hearts, to purify us, so that our words won't defile us or others. We ask You to help us to *"set a guard over our mouths, and keep watch over the door to our lips"* (Psalm 141:3, my paraphrase). Let us take to heart the many scriptures You gave us about the words we utter, so that like You, our words will bring forth life, and not death.

In Jesus' name,

Amen.

ENDNOTES:

1. https://americanvision.org/3880/jerusalem-mother-of-harlots/

Reflections on the Pittsburgh "Tree of Life" Synagogue Massacre

by Laura Densmore

*"My son, do not forget my law [Torah], But let your heart keep my commands;... She is a **Tree of Life** to those who take hold of her, and happy are all who retain her."* PROVERBS 3:1,18 (NKJV, emphasis mine)

In the year 1221, we read of an incident on The LIST in Erfurt Germany where anti-Jewish riots continued unabated by English crusaders. A group of religious "pilgrims" on their way to the Holy Land attacked the Jewish quarter and burned down two Jewish synagogues. Some 26 Jews were killed, while others threw themselves into the fire rather than be forcibly converted.

The only crime that these Jews committed was that they were worshiping the God of Israel in a synagogue, on the the Sabbath, according to their convictions in following the Hebrew Scriptures (the Torah). When I first read about this it felt like a sledgehammer hitting my spirit. This was done in the name of Christ? What an atrocity and an abomination! What a twisted and perverted distortion of who Yeshua truly is!

"Well", one might think, "that was the Dark Ages. That was nearly a thousand years ago when that happened. That could never happen in our modern times. We are enlightened now."

It is now with a heavy heart, and with tears that I pen these words.

Fast forward to Saturday morning, October 27th, 2018. News came through of a terrible shooting happening live at the Tree of Life Synagogue in Pittsburgh.[1]

The shooter, armed with an AR-15 assault rifle and two handguns, burst into the Tree of Life Jewish synagogue, yelling "All Jews must die". He began shooting people during their prayer service. Eleven people were slaughtered and killed, most of them over 55 years old.

Pictured above: Tree of Life Synagogue in Pittsburgh.

Jews are still being killed inside their houses of worship… even today.

I happened to be attending a Hebrew Roots congregation when the news of this terrible massacre came in during our own prayer service. I was horrified and cut to the heart to hear these words coming forth from one of the leaders:

> *"Well, you know those Jewish rabbis. They don't tell their people about the Messiah Yeshua. They aren't giving the people the truth. And, after all, there are people dying all the time. There are people dying in Chicago. We have people dying here in our own town. I read the obituaries every day, and I pray for the families of those who have passed on. We live in a fallen world and this is what sometimes happens."*

To hear these cold, callous, and unfeeling words coming from a leader, well, this was like salt on the wound.

I got up and walked out of the service in tears and began to pace in prayer out in the foyer. I had no words, only tears. How do you pray for a leader who speaks like this? The outrage shook my entire being. I began to pace and weep and pray and pace and weep and pray.

About a month later I had a meeting with him to have a conversation with him in the spirit of Matthew 18:15:

> *"Moreover if your brother sins against you, go and tell him his fault between you and him alone. If he hears you, you have gained your brother."* (NKJV)

With a broken heart, I let him know the effect his words had on me. I asked him why he had said those words? Did I misunderstand? Did he still stand by those words?

Regarding the Pittsburgh slaughter, he began to explain that when you are not in covenant with Yeshua, then you are out from under God's covering and protection and you are more prone to attacks from the enemy. This is what happens to you when you are "not saved". I asked him, *"Well then, what about all the Christian martyrs being beheaded and killed for their faith today in the Middle East?"*

He then asked me, *"Why do you think the Holocaust happened?"*

"Evil and sin was ruling through the Nazi regime and the seeds of Replacement Theology was bearing its evil fruit" I replied. I continued: *"Are you trying to say that this was God's punishment on the Jews, that they got their 'just rewards' because they are not in covenant with Yeshua?"*

He told me to go home and pray and ask the LORD to reveal to me what his true heart was concerning the Jews. That ended the conversation. I went home, broken-hearted.

As I reflected on what happened I began to see two things:

We need to lose the "us versus them" mindset. We must put away the "pointing of the finger." It is not "those people" in our history, who have done these wicked, evil and sinful things against the Jews. It is US. One of our own, Robert Bowers, a Christian nationalist, did this evil thing. The entry on *The LIST for Oct 27, 2018* reads:

> "Robert Bowers, a Christian nationalist with a deep hatred for Jews, yelled '*All Jews must die*' as he opened fire. In his bio section on the 'Gab' website (the alt-right version of Twitter), his profile photo caption reads *Jews are the children of Satan (John 8:44)*', adding '*The LORD Jesus Christ is come in the flesh.*'"

WE did it. This is OUR history. We must own it. We must own both the events and the mindsets that allowed those events to take place.

This atrocity committed in the name of Christ can serve as a clarion call to repentance to each and every one of us, from the greatest to the least, from leaders and teachers to every congregational member, from the top to bottom and from bottom to top. NO ONE is exempt. We ALL need to repent. And, if we think we don't have any sin to repent of, then perhaps we need to begin with repenting of pride.

> *"For the time is come that judgment must begin at the house of God: and if it **first begin at us**, what shall the end be of them that obey not the gospel of God?"* 1 PETER 4:17 (KJV, emphasis mine)

There are several stages that I have gone through in my own journey in repenting of the sins of my Church forefathers committed against the Jewish people:

1. First, I became aware of these sins (that's where The LIST came in). Then I had to take personal responsibility for them. I began by confessing these sins to the God of Israel and then entreating Him for the forgiveness of these sins.

2. Next, the spirit of God began turning my eyes and my heart towards Jerusalem, towards the Jewish people and towards the full counsel of the Word of God (from Genesis to Revelation).

3. Then, I began speaking out against any actions, words, or mindsets that would hurt, harm or undermine the Jewish people and/or the nation of Israel.

4. Finally, I began taking specific actions or a life work that in some way blesses the nation and people of Israel in the hopes that the Jewish people will see the change of heart now being reflected in my changed behavior. These "good deeds" demonstrate that the repentance has moved down from my heart to my feet (in actions and deeds). This sets up an environment for the possibility of walking side by side with the Jewish people in a spirit of love, cooperation and support.

As I reflect on the story that I have just shared with you, this was my own step three. It did take courage. There were risks involved — to my relationship with the leaders in this congregation. But, I could not be silent.

Would you pray this repentance prayer with me?

Abba, I am undone and broken of heart. Abba, I stand in the gap on behalf of my Hebrew roots community and I ask You to forgive us for these kinds of mindsets and attitudes that we are somehow morally and spiritually superior to the Jews because we have the salvation of Yeshua and they do not.

Abba, would You please forgive us for the "us versus them" mentality? May we put away the pointing of the finger of those people "out there" who have sinned, and may we begin with ourselves. May our hearts be broken and crushed with the things that break Your heart, O Abba! Would You break up the fallow ground of our hearts, Yeshua? Please send tears to water the hardened soil of our hearts!

Abba, please have mercy upon us. Abba, please take away our blindness. Abba, would You please have mercy upon this leader? For he is not alone. He stands alongside many pastors and leaders in the Church who would say the same. Abba, would You please send the gift of repentance from Your heart to him? Please send repentance to all of us! Please take away the scales that blind us. May our hearts be broken.

After prostrating ourselves before You, may we rise to stand with our Jewish brethren, love them, support them, stand beside them, and serve them, because truly they ARE our family. They are our long lost brothers and sisters. You love them, and so may we love whom You love. May the Jewish people find it in their hearts to forgive us and receive us. Abba, may You direct the building of the bridge and mortar us together with love.

In Yeshua's name,

Amen

ENDNOTES:

1. https://www.timesofisrael.com/at-least-11-killed-in-pittsburgh-synagogue-shooting/

2. https://www.theguardian.com/us-news/2018/oct/27/pittsburgh-synagogue-shooting

3. https://nypost.com/2018/10/27/shooter-screamed-all-jews-must-die-before-opening-fire-at-pittsburgh-synagogue/

Lively Stones: Building Walls?
Or Building Bridges?

by Laura Densmore

In 1241 CE, there was a pogrom in Frankfurt Germany (*see entry on The LIST, 1241*). This *Judenschlacht* (slaughter of the Jews) was sparked by the refusal of a Jew to convert to Christianity and resulted in the deaths of 180 Jews. Twenty-four Jews avoided death by accepting forced baptism. The synagogue was plundered and the Torah scrolls were destroyed.

Pope Gregory VII, the great reformer and organizer of the Church wrote in a letter to King Alfonse VI the following (*see entry on The LIST, 1081*):

"We exhort your Royal Majesty not to further tolerate that the Jews rule Christians and have power over them. For to allow that Christians are subordinated to Jews and are delivered to their whims means to oppress the Church of God, means to revile Christ Himself."

As we survey the bloody history of our Church forefathers, we see how wide and deep the chasm is between Jews and Christians. Our Church forefathers built a very high wall separating Jews from Christians. The wall was built brick by brick, stone by stone, with mindsets and actions.

"Therefore remember that you, once Gentiles in the flesh—who are called Uncircumcision by what is called the Circumcision made in the flesh by hands—that at that time you were without Christ, being aliens from the commonwealth of Israel and strangers from the covenants of promise,

having no hope and without God in the world. But now in Christ Jesus you who once were far off have been brought near by the blood of Christ. For He Himself is our peace, who has made both one, and has broken down the middle wall of separation." EPHESIANS 2:11-14 (KJV)

What is this wall of offense that has been there for centuries between Jews and Christians? What is the wall made of? How did it get built? And more importantly, how does the wall get dismantled?

As I pondered these questions, the Holy Spirit brought to my mind a vision. In this vision I saw many rectangular shaped tall standing stones. At first they were scattered all across a grassy pasture in disarray. Then men came and began moving them and placing them upright next to each other. One by one the stones were brought together. Mortar was placed between the stones. Slowly a stone wall was being erected. There were Christians on the far side of the wall and Jews on the near side of the wall. The wall continued to be constructed, getting higher and going out farther in both directions. Soon the wall was impassible. The wall stood strong and served to separate Jews from Christians for a long long time.

Then, in the next scene of the vision, I saw a Christian come and sit down at the base of the stone wall. He began to weep. He was repenting over the many sins done against the Jewish people. His heart was broken. Then, another Christian joined him. Then another. Soon there were many Christians on the far side of the wall, weeping. Some were pacing. Others were sitting. Many lay down on the grass with their faces to the ground, mourning and weeping.

As I watched, the mortar that kept the stones together began to melt and get soft and gooey. The stones were no longer held together with the mortar. The Christians on the far side of the wall, and the Jews on the near side of the wall began to knock down the stones so they were laying flat. The stone wall that had been there for so long was…. no more.

I saw at the edge of this grassy meadow a wild, raging river. No one had been able to cross to the other side because there was no bridge. Then, I saw the Jews and the Christians working together as they began moving the stones over to the river's edge. They laid the stones flat and began building a stone bridge across the river. The stones were the perfect building material to make this bridge. That was the end of the vision.

I inquired of the LORD and asked Him, *"What does this mean?"*

As I waited upon the LORD, the following scripture came to my mind:

Pictured above: Stone bridge crossing over the river.

"Ye also, as lively stones, are built up a spiritual house, an holy priesthood, to offer up spiritual sacrifices, acceptable to God by Jesus Christ. Wherefore also it is contained in the scripture, Behold, I lay in Zion a chief cornerstone, elect, and precious: and he that believes on him shall not be confounded."
1 PETER 2:5-6 (KJV)

Here is what I sensed was the "interpretation" of the vision:

Each one of us is a "lively stone" or a "living stone." The lively stones represent people. The chief cornerstone is Yeshua. Now, if each stone, representing a person, decides to stand up tall, then these stones begin to form a wall.

The stones standing upright represents pride, spiritual superiority and self righteousness. The wall was built when our Church forefathers stood tall in pride.

To dismantle the wall, the people of God must repent of pride.

"For You do not desire sacrifice, or else I would give it; The sacrifices of God are a broken spirit, A broken and a contrite heart—These, O God, You will not despise. PSALM 51:16-17 (NKJV)

When the people of God begin to humble themselves and repent of the sins of our Church forefathers, this represents the lively stones lying down FLAT. And the wall, which has been built up over the centuries, gets dismantled.

Instead of standing upright and tall, the "lively stones" take up this new position to lie down prone, in humility and repentance. The mortar melts.

THEN the Master builder, the God of Israel, directs the building of the stone bridge across the river.

Could it be that this bridge must be finished before the Messiah can come, the bridge over which He will walk as we prepare the way for Him?

Will you pray this repentance prayer with me?

Abba, would You please establish a new posture and a new mindset in us? We are broken and undone over the sin of our Church forefathers. We humble ourselves. We repent of the pride and spiritual superiority.

Abba, we no longer wish to stand tall in pride. We lay ourselves before You, prostrate and undone.

Abba, have mercy.

Abba, forgive.

Abba, in Your kindness and mercy and grace, would You please use each of us to be a "lively stone" to build out the bridge between Jews and Christians?

How can we serve our Jewish brothers and sisters? How can we support them and be a blessing to them? That is where we must begin.

And in the midst of everything You call us to do, please help us to walk in love, honor and respect for our Jewish brothers and sisters.

In Yeshua's name,

Amen!

From Fast Day to Feast Day!

by Bob O'Dell

Five days before the 9th of Av in 2018, I heard Christian leader Christine Darg tell the Speaker of the Israel Knesset Yuli Edelstein that she visits Jerusalem every year on the 9th of Av, in the hope of personally witnessing the moment the prophecy will be fulfilled *that the fast day of the 9th of Av will one day become a feast day* for the Jewish people.

Two days later, I was on a phone call with Orthodox Jew Eliyahu Berkowitz of Breaking Israel News, being interviewed about the implications of publishing The LIST and the meeting two days prior with Speaker Yuli Edelstein. Eliyahu is known for his thousands of articles written on the topic of redemption and the coming of the Messianic Age. He said he was not particularly interested in having Christians grovel in self-deprecation for the sins of our past that we are unable to fix, and asked about the mood of the meeting with Yuli. I responded saying:

"There seemed to be a lot of joy in that room."

After further questioning and reflection he pronounced his opinion:

"I think that what you are doing here is creating a Christian 9th of Av. What do you think?"

I responded:

"How should I know? We are just trying to put one foot in front of the other! I don't think it is our place to pronounce such a thing."

In the end Eliyahu did not include his comment in the article, but it certainly got me thinking.

Then, on the 9th of Av in 2018, five years after first reading through the list of atrocities, one minute-at-a-time, I read through the list a second time.

Late in that summer day, I sat down outside to listen to a podcast replay of a sermon from Pastor Trey Graham, of Melissa Texas, who earlier that day had (amazingly) delivered a sermon to his church about the 9th of Av. His sermon began with Kadesh Barnea and the spiritual warfare that must have been present to encourage the ten spies to give a bad report. But his sermon ended by reading two passages from Zechariah 8, that were going to rock my world. We will talk about the first passage in this devotional, and save the second passage for my final devotional.

Let's set the stage for what he read.

The seventy-year Babylonian exile of the Jewish people had ended. During that period a fast in Babylon had been instituted on the 9th of Av to mourn the destruction of the First Temple. But now that the Temple was being rebuilt, men from the town of Bethel came to inquire of the priests about whether they should continue to fast and weep on the 9th of Av, as they had in the past? I agree that this was an excellent question! The Lord's response to them in Zechariah 7:5 probably surprised them. He began with a rather harsh question, *"Was it actually for Me that you fasted?"*

> *"Speak unto all the people of the land, and to the priests, saying, When ye fasted and mourned in the fifth and seventh month, even those seventy years, did ye at all fast unto me, even to me?"* ZECHARIAH 7:5 (KJV)

From this opening it would soon be clear that the answer was going to be "No! Do not stop fasting!" Then after further discourse the Lord declares that something much bigger and better is going to come in the future than what they were currently witnessing. The Lord would bring about a return to the land of Israel that would be much larger, and would come about with great salvation and blessing. The Lord then spoke the words that the Pastor would read on that Sunday, the words shown in the photo (next page).

Now I have one more person to bring into the story: Rabbi Tuly Weisz. While I would not learn about this until weeks later in the Sukkot holidays, Rabbi Tuly Weisz of Israel 365 had been touched by the knowledge of the work we were doing. He delivered a talk to his own synagogue on the day before the 9th of Av. Later he recorded a talk for us[1], to explain his thinking, saying:

> *"This past Tisha B'Av I noticed that the fast of the 5th month is actually Av. What does it mean that these days shall become joy and gladness? Because*

Pictured above: Original photo by Bob O'Dell of Western wall overlaid with scripture from Zechariah 8:19

there is an idea in Judaism that one day there will not be any holidays at all — they will be cancelled. Yet it seems that the prophet Zechariah is going out of his way to say that the fast days are not going to be cancelled — they will be transformed into days of feasts and festivals.

Why would the holidays, for instance Passover, be cancelled? We know it will be cancelled because in Jeremiah 16:14 it says:

> *"Assuredly, a time is coming—declares Hashem—when it shall no more be said, 'As Hashem lives who brought the Israelites out of the land of Egypt,' but rather, 'As Hashem lives who brought the Israelites out of the northland, and out of all the lands to which He had banished them.' For I will bring them back to their land, which I gave to their fathers."*
> JEREMIAH 16:14-15 (THE ISRAEL BIBLE)

Based on this, the Jewish belief is that there will not be a Passover; that because we will be so close to God, we will not need the holidays to direct our attention to God in that moment in time. The same is believed for Shavuot and a Sukkot. So then why does Jeremiah declare the fast days will become feast days?

Here is what I believe. Each of the different fast days will eventually correspond to a different Jewish Holiday. I believe that it will be the holiday of Passover which will be replaced by the 9th of Av, which has inside of it the correcting [or redemption] of those tragic incidents in Jewish history."

What I hear Rabbi Tuly saying here is that the miracle of the Feast of Passover and Unleavened Bread, that instituted the great Exodus to the Promised Land, can be seen as somewhat tarnished by the later, horrific destruction of the Temples and many exiles and Jewish expulsions. Tuly believes that when Jeremiah 16:14-15 is finally and completely fulfilled, then the mighty Exodus from Egypt and its associated Passover, will itself be overshadowed by an even greater Exodus event which will occur on the 9th of Av!

Rabbi Tuly continues:

> *"The only thing that can bring about that redemption and transformation from fast to feast is through repentance. On the 9th of Av the Jewish people sit on the floor and we repent. We cry. We are broken. We try to get closer to God. We consider what led to the destruction of the Temple and how we can bring about the rebuilding of the Temple. It is a very internal process and we try to repent as much as we can.*
>
> *But, I believe that because these fast days in Jewish history were all brought about by the enemies of the Jewish people, in some way, shape or form, then what will trigger the fast day to become the feast day?* **It will happen when not only do the Jewish people repent on the 9th of Av, but when non-Jewish people repent as well.** *Anybody who takes the Bible seriously needs to take the Jewish festivals seriously. And when the non-Jewish world starts to understand that these Biblical holidays are part of the Biblical story, and begins to take the Biblical fast days seriously and to participate in the fast days and to repent on them, in that way God will bring about turning the fast days into feast days.*
>
> *So to have non-Jews commemorating the 9th of Av for the first time in history — it has never happened before that more and more non-Jews are participating in the 9th of Av, owning their role, not a personal role but a spiritual role in the 9th of Av — I pray that this becomes the trigger to turn the fast into feast, and [to continue to advance] that spiritual revolution, the redemption of Israel described in Jeremiah, that is now happening.*
>
> *I am so moved that there are non-Jewish people who are connecting with the 9th of Av and repenting on the 9th of Av. May God hear all of our prayers, and all of our repentance."*

We are so blessed to record these words of Rabbi Tuly in this devotional. But is not the Feast of Passover a week-long celebration rather than just a single day? That topic will be addressed in this book's final devotion.

Will you pray this repentance prayer with me?

Father in Heaven,

Thank You for the Jewish people. Thank You for the long and continuous history of faithfulness that You have shown to the Jewish people through their many destructions, exiles and expulsions. Thank You for Jews who are willing to declare, explain, and undergird that which we sense you calling US to do, as being part of the process of the redemption of Israel. Thank You for declaring that even the darkest of all fast days — the 9th of Av — will one day become a feast day.

We pray right along with the Rabbi, and say to You also: May You LORD God, King of the Universe, hear all of our prayers and all of our repentance.

Amen.

ENDNOTES:

1. https://youtu.be/oY95hdU-c4c

Jews Are a Blessing

by Ray Montgomery

"I will make you a great nation, I will bless you.
I will make your name great, and you will be a blessing."
GENESIS 12:2 (GWT)

Lyman Abbott (1835-1921), American preacher and journalist, wrote:[1]

"We Gentiles owe our life to Israel.

It is Israel who has brought us the message that God is one and that God is a just and a righteous God and demands righteousness of His children, and demands nothing else.

It is Israel that has brought us the message that God is our Father.

It is Israel who, in bringing us the divine Law, has laid the foundation of liberty.

It is Israel who had the first free institutions the world ever saw.

It is Israel who has brought us our Bible, our prophets, our apostles.

When sometimes our own unchristian prejudices flame out against the Jewish people, let us remember that all that we have and all that we are, we owe under God, to what Judaism has given us."

If ever there were a people who should bear a grudge against Christians for how they have been mistreated (as extensively revealed in The LIST), it is the Jews. And yet time and time again, I am struck by how warmly I have been received, both one-on-one, and as a guest into their synagogues.

I have been changed not only by my research into Jewish history, but also by my personal interaction with Jews, and hearing many testimonies from Holocaust survivors, mostly at the Los Angeles Museum of the Holocaust, or at Christians United for Israel (CUFI) sponsored events, where even this stony-hearted, somewhat cynical man (in those days) was profoundly moved to tears.

In 2013 I was living in Lancaster, California, and wanted to attend a synagogue. I informed the Rabbi I was a Christian, but that I wasn't there to proselytise; I was there to learn and to see how Jews interpret scripture. I was at once struck by how warmly I was welcomed into their congregation. People were not only friendly, but they seemed to genuinely care for each other, with a warmth and genuineness I haven't seen in any church I have ever attended.

But consider Jewish achievements on a wider, global scale, which are out of all proportion to the size of their population. I studied classical music at University, but even as a teenager I noticed a disproportionate number of world-class musicians — relative to population — who have been Jews. Jews comprise less than 0.2% of the world's population,[2] yet they have received more than 22.5% of all Nobel prizes ever awarded.[3] Israel itself comprises only 0.11% of the world's population,[4] yet in March 2019, she was listed as the world's eighth most powerful country for the third consecutive year![5]

I subscribe to nocamels.com, a website covering Israeli research and innovation in technology, medicine, design and the environment, and I am constantly inspired by what is happening there. Israel is now the world's number one start-up nation,[6] with Beersheba being the new Silicon Valley.[7]

Israel successfully launched a spacecraft on February 21st, 2019 which is set to land on the Moon on April 11th,[8] which, if successful (God willing), will make it the fourth country in history to do so. In just 70 short years, Israel has gone from scratch – to landing on the Moon! *Extraordinary!!*

Perhaps what I am trying to say is how profoundly I have been changed by Jews' achievements and my interactions with them personally. Perhaps we should hear from those who are far more literate than I can ever be, and who can express it far more eloquently than I ever could, as to why Jews are a blessing to the world:

John Adams (1735-1826), 2nd President of the United States:[9]

"I will insist that the Hebrews have done more to civilize men than any other nation. If I were an atheist, and believed in blind eternal fate, I should still believe that fate had ordained the Jews to be the most essential instrument for civilizing the nations.

If I were an atheist of the other sect, who believe or pretend to believe that all is ordered by chance, I should believe that chance had ordered the Jews to preserve and propagate to all mankind the doctrine of a supreme, intelligent, wise, almighty sovereign of the universe, which I believe to be the great essential principle of all morality, and consequently of all civilization."

Leo Tolstoy (1828-1910), Russian icon of nonviolent resistance, author, social reformer:[1]

"What is a Jew? This question is not at all so odd as it seems. Let us see what kind of peculiar creature the Jew is, which all the rulers and all the nations have together and separately abused and molested, oppressed and persecuted, trampled and butchered, burned and hanged... and in spite of all this is yet alive!

What is a Jew, who has never allowed himself to be led astray by all the earthly possessions which his oppressors and persecutors constantly offered him in order that he should change his faith and forsake his own Jewish religion?

The Jew is that sacred being who has brought down from the heaven the everlasting fire and has illuminated with it the entire world. He is the religious source, spring and fountain out of which all the rest of the peoples have drawn their beliefs and their religions...

The Jew is the emblem of eternity. He whom neither slaughter nor torture of thousands of years could destroy, he whom neither fire nor sword nor inquisition was able to wipe off the face of the earth, he who was the first to produce the Oracles of God, he who has been for so long the guardian of the prophecy, and who transmitted it to the rest of the world – such a nation cannot be destroyed. The Jew is as everlasting as is eternity itself."

Mark Twain (1835-1910), author, humorist:[1]

"If the statistics are right, the Jews constitute but one percent of the human race. It suggests a nebulous dim puff of stardust lost in the blaze of the Milky Way. Properly the Jew ought hardly to be heard of; but he is heard of, has always been heard of. He is as prominent on the planet as any other people, and his commercial importance is extravagantly out of proportion to the

smallness of his bulk. His contributions to the world's list of great nations in literature, science, art, music, finance, medicine, and abstruse learning, are also way out of proportion to the weakness of his numbers. He has made a marvelous fight in this world, in all the ages; and has done it with his hands tied behind him. He could be vain of himself, and be excused for it.

The Egyptian, the Babylonian, and the Persian rose, filled the planet with sound and splendor, then faded to dream-stuff and passed away; the Greeks and Romans followed, and made a vast noise, and they are gone; other peoples have sprung up and held their torch high for a time, but it burned out, and they sit in twilight now, or have vanished.

The Jews saw them all, beat them all, and is now what he always was, exhibiting no decadence, no infirmities of age, no weakening of his parts, no slowing of his energies, no dulling of his alert and aggressive mind.

All things are mortal but the Jew; all other forces pass, but he remains. What is the secret of his immortality?"

Pictured above: Torah scroll of the Hebrew scriptures

But we shouldn't forget the two greatest blessings of all that they have given us. The first is the Tanakh, the Hebrew scriptures which Christians call the Old Testament, faithfully and meticulously copied from year-to-year, century-to-century, for millennia. They are also inviting us to study the scriptures with them, with the publication of the Israel Bible. The online publication allows us to not only see the Hebrew scriptures side-by-side with the English translation, but also to hear how the Hebrew scriptures sound.[10]

And finally, for Christians, they have given us our Jewish Messiah Yeshua, and the New Testament. Now that's something to shout Hallelujah from the rooftops for!

Will you prayer of praise and thanksgiving with me?

Heavenly Father,

We ask for forgiveness for the awful responsibility we bear as Christians for the mistreatment of Your chosen people over the millennia by our Church forefathers. We are humbled by the example of grace, mercy, forgiveness, love, and absence of retribution they have shown us in return. We acknowledge that they truly have become a blessing to the world, and a light unto the nations.

We stand in awe at Your restoration of Israel as a nation, and we thank You for their contributions to science, the arts, and more. We commit to standing by Your people from this day forward, in word and deed. Let us bless them, beginning with making restitution for the sins we have perpetrated against them. And by so doing, we ask that You continue to join us together in unity, Your chosen people, with we who have been graciously grafted in.

In Jesus' name,

Amen.

ENDNOTES:

1. http://jewsforjudaism.org/knowledge/articles/quotes-about-the-jewish-people/

2. https://www.ynetnews.com/articles/0,7340,L-4291987,00.html

3. https://en.wikipedia.org/wiki/List_of_Jewish_Nobel_laureates

4. http://www.worldometers.info/world-population/israel-population/

5. https://www.jns.org/israel-ranked-eighth-most-powerful-country-in-world/
   https://www.usnews.com/news/best-countries/power-rankings?fbclid=IwAR0H93
   OHs3QgPEZ0erqvd8-MOwFIBPwkUB6h53GYYiw6FYJo3aupuvzOY7U

6. https://www.forbes.com/sites/startupnationcentral/2018/05/14/israeli-techs-identity-crisis-startup-nation-or-scale-up-nation/#3daafdaaef48

7. http://e.forbes.co.il/a-new-silicon-valley-in-the-middle-east-beer-sheva-rising/

8. https://www.space.com/israel-lunar-lander-long-trip-moon.html?utm_source=sdc-newsletter&utm_medium=email&utm_campaign=20190223-sdc

9. http://www.jewishencyclopedia.com/articles/767-adams-john

10. https://theisraelbible.com/bible

On the 9th of Av, A Prophetic Declaration: Two Temples Destroyed, One Temple Designed

by Ray Montgomery

"But the men who had gone up with him said, 'We can't attack those people; they are stronger than we are.' And they spread among the Israelites a bad report about the land they have explored..." NUMBERS 13:31-32 (NIV)

The 9th of Av has traditionally been a day of tragedy for Israel, and its roots go back to Kadesh Barnea, when 10 of the 12 spies came back with a negative report. As a result, that entire generation, except for Joshua and Caleb, died in the wilderness and never made it into the Promised Land:

"No one from this evil generation shall see the good land I swore to give your ancestors," DEUTERONOMY 1:35 (NIV)

According to Rabbinic tradition, the sin of the spies produced the annual fast day of Tisha B'Av, or the 9th of Av. By accepting the false report, they wept over the false idea that God was setting them up for defeat. The night they cried was the 9th of Av, which has since been a day of weeping — and misfortune — for the Jews.

The following tragedies occurred on the 9th of Av (*see all entries on The LIST for their respective years*):

586 BCE   The First Temple: destroyed

70 CE   The Second Temple: destroyed

71	The Romans plow Jerusalem over with salt
130	Hadrian orders Governor Rufus to plow Jerusalem over
135	The Fall of Betar, the last stronghold of Jewish leaders
136	Jerusalem is rebuilt as the Roman city of Aelia Capitolina
1096	Pope Urban II declared the start of the First Crusade
1290	Jews expelled from England
1492	Jews expelled from Spain
1555	Papal Bull of Pope Paul IV confines Jews into a walled ghetto in Rome
1626	Sabbatai Zevi is born, who later claimed to be the Jewish Messiah
1648	The Cossacks massacre thousands of East European Jews
1914	World War I begins
1941	Himmler receives approval for the "Final Solution" of the Jews
1942	Treblinka extermination camp opens in Poland
2005	Forced evacuation of Jews from Gaza is *scheduled* — but postponed until the next day

It should be noted that many of those tragedies were perpetrated by our Church forefathers!

Pictured above: Screen shot from the video "The Children are Ready" (2012),[1] produced by The Temple Institute.

But in 2012 the Temple Institute, a Jewish organisation dedicated to the vision of building a Third Temple, began releasing annual "Tisha B'Av" videos. The first three were aptly titled "The Children are Ready", and feature children building models of the Third Temple,[1,2] or children looking over at the Temple Mount where the Temple is under construction.[3] Then in 2015, in the weeks leading up to the 9th of Av, the Temple Institute said they had an important announcement to make. On that day they released a video announcing to the world that the "architectural plans for the Third Temple have begun!"[4]

It was on the 9th of Av that the First and Second Temples were destroyed, so how fitting that the Temple Institute released architectural plans to rebuild the Temple: *on the 9th of Av!* Could it be that this day of destruction, loss, grief and sorrow could soon become a day of blessing and celebration?

Pictured above: Screen shot from the video The Children are Ready (2014),[3] produced by The Temple Institute.

The prophetic import of this announcement cannot be overstated. First, instead of focusing on the negative events in history, it becomes a positive event that, in effect, says "Enough! We are now looking to the future." Second, the litany of tragic events that began with the destruction of both the First and Second Temples, is now counterbalanced by the release of architectural blueprints for the Third Temple. And finally, it announced to the world that the stage is now set for rebuilding the Temple, something the Temple Institute has been working on for the last three decades.

In the Temple Institute's own words:[5]

> *"An awareness of the historical inevitability and the spiritual necessity of the Third Temple has reentered the consciousness of the Jewish people... the movement of Jews back into the history of their people is a growing tide*

that cannot be stemmed. A great responsibility has been returned to our hands. The keys that the priests returned to the safekeeping of heaven on that terrible 9th of Av 1,941 years ago have been thrust back into our hands. G-d has entrusted us with our own fate — and with His future — as it were — on this earth. We must understand that the fast days of our times are the very last fast days to be. We have been blessed with the ability to make this happen. We have been entrusted with the responsibility to see to it that it happens. The days of mourning, the destruction of the second Temple have ended. The days of mourning our own lethargy regarding the Third Temple will soon be over. The time has arrived to effect the tikkun — the repair — and to establish the 9th of Av as a day of rejoicing forever. The choice is ours — if only we close ranks, and unite to make it happen."

The Temple Institute, founded in 1987, has been collecting and constructing all the vessels required for Temple service, such as recreating the golden menorah, the table of showbread, making the High Priest's garments, and so on. In partnership with the Temple Institute, Harrari Harps has been building harps and lyres necessary for Temple worship, including King David's 10-string harp, which one rabbi said was a sign we had entered the Messianic Age.

Another such "sign" is the rediscovery in the 1990s of the source of the blue dye used in the fringes of the tallit (the Jewish prayer shawl) and the High Priest's tunic: the Murex sea snail, whose purple dye, *when exposed to the sun,* turns blue. In 2004 the Sanhedrin was re-established, and in 2011 the Temple Institute released blueprints for the Sanhedrin Assembly Hall and the Chamber of Hewn Stone, which will form part of the Temple complex itself.

Subsequently, with the announcement of the Third Temple Plans on the 9th of Av in 2015 (*see entry on The LIST, 2015*), there now seems to be a wave of building momentum that cannot be stopped:

- 2015: the Temple Institute began breeding Red Angus cattle with the hopes of eventually raising a perfect red heifer, whose ashes will be required by priests for purification purposes.

- 2016: the nascent Sanhedrin appointed a High Priest, and opened a school in Jerusalem to train Levite priests for Third Temple service.

- 2016: the silver half-shekel Temple tax was re-introduced by the nascent Sanhedrin. Proceeds will go towards priestly training and the recreation of special vessels and utensils for Temple use.

- 2017: President Trump recognized Jerusalem as Israel's capital.

- 2018: President Trump moved the US Embassy from Tel Aviv to Jerusalem on May 14th, Israel's 70th anniversary.

- 2018: In December, Rabbi Yosef Berger, the rabbi of King David's Tomb on Mount Zion, initiated a special project to create a golden crown to be presented to the Messiah-King upon his arrival in Jerusalem.

With trained "Cohen" priests, direct descendants from the family of Aaron, now practising and re-enacting the sacrificial rites associated with Temple worship, many are saying that the stage is now truly set for the Messianic Age to begin. And with these preparations in place, and as the 2015 Temple Institute announcement declares: the Third Temple is becoming a reality in our time!

Will you pray this repentance prayer with me?

Heavenly Father,

We repent for the historic role our Church forefathers played in creating tragedy for our Jewish brethren on the 9th of Av, and we ask for Your forgiveness. We acknowledge that fear and unbelief caused an entire generation to miss out on moving into the Promised Land, which became the basis for this historical pattern of tragedy to befall the Jews. We repent of these sins too, and ask for Your forgiveness. And if we have been guilty of allowing fear and unbelief to settle in our own hearts and minds, likewise impeding us from moving into all that you have purposed in our lives, we confess that as sin, and ask for Your forgiveness.

With this repentance, would You please redeem the 9th of Av, and turn this tragic day of mourning into a day of joy, celebration, and anticipation?

Our Christian past is littered with examples of our taking offense at the Jews for the things they believe and the things they do. Let us not repeat the mistakes of the past. Almighty God, we pray that we would not stand against Your will in the future, as we have in the past. So regarding the building of the Third Temple we strongly declare: "Thy will be done, Oh Lord!"

We look forward to that day when Yeshua will be seated upon His Throne in Jerusalem. We look forward to the prophetic fulfillment of Yeshua's proclamation about the Temple becoming "a house of prayer for all nations".

In Jesus' name,

Amen.

ENDNOTES:

1. https://www.youtube.com/watch?v=LPmViwmJSJE

2. https://www.youtube.com/watch?v=5bw-lJlyuqA

3. https://www.youtube.com/watch?v=B6C_zfpEwUI

4. https://www.youtube.com/watch?v=A2IkxmwkayM

5. http://www.templeinstitute.org/time_to_build.htm

Redeeming the Sin of the Ten Spies

by Bob O'Dell

In my first devotional, *Undone*, I told you the story of the 9th of Av in 2013, and how that experience led me to meet Gidon on the walls of Jerusalem, hear his vision for what is now Root Source, and help him get his vision up and running. Then in a more recent devotional, *From Fast Day to Feast Day,* I told you how I heard Pastor Trey Graham read those verses in Zechariah about the fast day of the 9th of Av becoming a feast day in the future. He read:

> *"Then the word of the Lord of hosts came to me, saying, 'Thus says the Lord of hosts, the fast of the fourth, and the fast of the fifth [the 9th of Av], and the fast of the seventh, and the fast of the tenth months will become joy, gladness, and cheerful feasts for the house of Judah; so love truth and peace.'"*
> ZECHARIAH 8:18-19 (NASB)

In that same devotional Rabbi Tuly Weisz told us how Christian involvement in the 9th of Av might trigger the transition of the 9th of Av from fast day to feast day. He said:

> *"But, I believe that because these fast days in Jewish history were all brought about by the enemies of the Jewish people, in some way, shape or form, then what will trigger the fast day to become the feast day? **It will happen when not only do the Jewish people repent on the 9th of Av, but when non-Jewish people repent as well.**"*

I will now finish the story of what happened to me on the 9th of Av, 2018 in my backyard.

When I heard Pastor Trey read that verse from Zechariah, my ears jumped at the phrase: "for the house of **Judah**".

We who are Christians see ourselves as spiritually grafted into Israel, but this particular promise of "fast day to feast day" was not given to all of Israel, but specifically to the house of Judah. I began to wonder if God might be saying that because we, as Christians, perpetrated most of the evil against the Jews over the last 2,000 years, that perhaps it was our turn to take ahold of this day ourselves, as a perpetual day of fasting and remembrance!

In the days ahead when the 9th of Av becomes a day of feasting for Jews, might we in the Christian world still need to retain it as a day of remembrance and resolve never to turn against our Jewish brothers again? I recalled what Eliyahu Berkowitz had told me just three days earlier, *"I think you might be creating a Christian 9th of Av."* Was Eliyahu right?

This insight alone would have been enough for me on the 9th of Av in 2018, but God had more! Trey did not stop reading at Zechariah 8:19, but kept reading to the end of the chapter! He read through to verse 23:

> *"Thus says the Lord of hosts, 'It will yet be that peoples will come, even the inhabitants of many cities. The inhabitants of one will go to another, saying, "Let us go at once to entreat the favor of the Lord, and to seek the Lord of hosts; I will also go." So many peoples and mighty nations will come to seek the Lord of hosts in Jerusalem and to entreat the favor of the Lord.' Thus says the Lord of hosts, 'In those days ten men from all the nations will grasp the garment of a Jew, saying, "Let us go with you, for we have heard that God is with you."'"* (NASB)

I see a three-stage process in those verses:

1. In stage one, the peoples and inhabitants of many cities will feel a sense of urgency to entreat the favor of the LORD and to seek him. Individuals will make their own decisions to go or not go. **It was a personal decision to GO DO something.**

2. In stage two, many peoples and mighty nations will come to seek the LORD of hosts in Jerusalem and to entreat the favor of the LORD. **Groups of people now come to Jerusalem together to entreat the favor of the LORD.**

3. Finally in stage three, ten persons from the nations will grasp the garment of a Jew saying to that Jew: *"Let us go with you, because God [Elohim] is with you."* **This verse reveals to us that the joining of ten persons from the nations to one Jew happens in Jerusalem.**

When I heard those words in my backyard, particularly the final sentence, my jaw dropped. I knew that verse well, but I had never once thought about the ten men grabbing onto a Jew *in Jerusalem.* After five years of having my heart turned towards the Orthodox Jews of Israel, it finally dawned on me that *I had gone through this three-stage process personally.* In stage one, I was undone on the 9th of Av in 2013. I felt a sense of urgency, but I had no answers.

In stage two, I made a decision to go to Jerusalem, without a clear idea of what that "looked like". Without a clear plan I pushed back against my fear of failure and went anyway in January 2014. Then in stage three, on that very trip, as part of a Christian prayer meeting *in Jerusalem*, I happened to meet Gidon Ariel on the walls of the Old City of Jerusalem where he shared his vision. The exact words the Holy Spirit spoke to me at that moment were: "That's your man!"

There in my backyard I then saw that Zechariah 8:23 told me that I should NOT be the only Christian grabbing on to Gidon! There should be ten of us! I began to imagine how beautiful it would be if Christians worldwide were to come to Jerusalem, meet Jews in Jerusalem, and for the Holy Spirit to say to *them*, just like He did to *me*: "That's the Jew I want you to walk beside!" I was now in tears.

This "grabbing on" idea made perfect sense, because my own experience showed that **only when we repent** can we have the right heart attitude in our relationships with Jews. If we haven't repented, we can easily feel superior and attempt to dominate or control.

But even that insight was not the climactic moment on my 9th of Av. The LORD still had one more surprise. He caused my mind to recall how Pastor Trey Graham had begun his 9th of Av sermon with the incident of the twelve spies at Kadesh Barnea, and the ten spies who gave an evil report of the land.

Do you see where I am heading, dear reader? Stop reading and ponder what God was about to reveal!

Selah.

I was undone once again on the 9th of Av. It was beyond all expectation!

Pictured above: Finishing the 40-day repentance journey.

We Christians, by repenting on the 9th of Av, by coming to Jerusalem, and by having ten of us grab onto the hem of the garment of a Jew, **not only help fulfill the biblical prophecy of Zechariah 8:18-23**, but we, by being spiritually grafted into Israel, **can redeem the sin of the ten spies** on the 9th of Av at Kadesh Barnea as well!

Selah.

In Conclusion

This is the 40th day of this devotional journey. The first devotion spoke about the evil report of the ten spies at Kadesh Barnea. This, our last devotion, takes us back to Kadesh Barnea, now casting a vision of how we might actually help to redeem it — in Jerusalem.

Today is the 9th of Av. It is not just a day for the Jews, it is a day for Christians as well.

Many stories in this book described sons and daughters who are now redeeming the sins of their forefathers.

The story of Kadesh Barnea is a story of unbelief and an evil report. This sin applies to all Christians. May we all step into God's story, into history and into the future, by taking the 9th of Av seriously, by finding it in our hearts to come to Jerusalem, and by being open to grab the hem of a certain Jew to whom the Spirit of God might lead.

This is the heart of the idea for what we are calling The Nations' Ninth of Av. We come to Jerusalem, not just for that one day, but for one week to allow Christians to meet Jews that they never knew, to see how God might move upon those Christians. Will some of them grab ahold of the hem of a Jew, and walk along beside them?

When ten grab on to a Jew, that makes eleven! I asked Gidon Ariel what he thinks about that? He told me:

> *"All eleven still need a leader. For Christians that leader will certainly be Yeshua. For us, I suppose it is Joshua. But in any case, we are going to have to walk together in a bit of a mystery, are we not?"*

Yes we are!

Will you pray this prayer of praise and thanksgiving with me?

Father in Heaven,

Oh the depth of the riches both of the wisdom and knowledge of God!

How unsearchable are Your judgments and unfathomable are Your ways!

For who has known the mind of the LORD, or who became His counselor?

Or who has given to You that it might be paid back to us again?

For from You and through You and to You are all things!

To You be the Glory forever.

Amen!

Yom Kippur Repentance Prayer

by Cathy Helms

Holy One of Israel, our hearts are rent, with faces covered with shame and hands stained with innocent blood. With faces to the ground, we bow before You to plead for mercy. We declare that You are our God and we are Your people. We declare that there is no other God. We present ourselves before You today, on Yom Kippur 2019, to confess our grievous sin against You, Yehovah, Elohim of Israel: our rebellion, transgression, and iniquity, and that of our Church forefathers.

Give ear, O Shepherd of Israel, to our humble cry for restoration both to You and to our brother, Judah. We have heard Your voice calling to us:

> *"Return, O Israel, to the LORD your God, for you have stumbled because of your iniquity. Take with you words and return to the LORD; say to him, 'Take away all iniquity; accept what is good, and we will pay with bulls the vows of our lips.'"* HOSEA 14:1-2 (ESV)

With faces to the ground, we respond to Your most gracious invitation, and indeed we beg: please take away our iniquity! We are murderers and liars, guilty of everything that You call abomination.

Your offer to forgive us and cleanse us has given us the courage to appear before You.

> *"I said, How I would set you among my sons, and give you a pleasant land, a heritage most beautiful of all nations..."* JEREMIAH 3:19 (ESV)

As we have begun to wake from our long sleep, it has dawned upon us that we are the prodigal son of Luke 15 who went into a far country, despised Your instruction, and squandered our inheritance.

Your invitation to call You "Father" has humbled and broken us.

> *"And I thought you would call me, My Father, and would not turn from following me."* JEREMIAH 3:19 (ESV)

Therefore, with hearts rent by Your lovingkindness which endures forever, and Your promise to Abraham, Isaac, and Jacob that their descendants would be as the sand of the sea, we cry with deep gratitude:

"Abba, Father, thank You for sending Your Son, Yeshua, the Lamb of God, to redeem us with His blood, to cleanse us from all sin and iniquity, to take us to be His bride, that we might be joint heirs with Him. And thank You for sending Your Holy Spirit into our hearts, to bring to our remembrance Your Torah of life, wisdom, shalom, and blessing, so that we are no longer slaves to sin." Galatians 4:4-6; John 14:26; Deuteronomy 28:1-13; Romans 8:17

You have graciously enlarged our hearts to understand the Hebrew Scriptures as our rightful and precious heritage, as well as that of our Jewish brothers, and, therefore, a sure foundation and a fountain of wisdom. We repent for our forefathers' claims that Your holy instruction was done away with or lacks relevance to us. We now understand that Israel, the intended holy nation and bride of Yeshua, is meant to model Your great wisdom, by keeping Your commandments, in step with the Bridegroom, being led by the Holy Spirit, that the nations might be provoked by jealousy to also enter into covenant with You.

"For what great nation is there that has a god so near to it as the LORD our God is to us, whenever we call upon him? And what great nation is there, that has statutes and rules so righteous as all this law that I set before you today?" DEUTERONOMY 4:7, 8 (ESV)

Because You have removed our blindness we now see the entire bible is Good News from Genesis through Revelation, which You are writing upon our hearts. Your Word, Your Covenant, and Your Torah are echad, or One, as You and Yeshua are One, and as You desire us to be one with Him in order to draw all peoples and nations to You.

If indeed Your anger has indeed turned from us, have mercy upon us and our children! Heal our apostasy and love us freely! (Hosea 14:4). We see that our ancestors are the people whom You called "Jezreel", or "Scattered" (Hosea 1:4), "Lo Ruhamah" or "No Mercy" (Hosea 1:6), and "Lo Ami" or "Not My people" (Hosea 1:9).

Yet, You have promised:

"I will betroth you to me in faithfulness. And you shall know the LORD."
HOSEA 2:20 (ESV)

*"...And I will have mercy on **No Mercy**, and I will say to **Not My People**, 'You are my people' and he shall say, 'You are my God.'"* HOSEA 2:23 (ESV, emphases mine); *also* 1 PETER 2:10, ROMANS 11:30

Indeed, Holy One of Israel, we do hereby stand before You and declare:

"I have heard Ephraim grieving, 'You have disciplined me, and I was disciplined, like an untrained calf; bring me back that I may be restored, for you are the LORD my God." JEREMIAH 31:18 (ESV)

We declare You alone are our Elohim, *"the great and awesome God who keeps covenant and steadfast love with those who love Him and keep His commandments."* Daniel 9:4 (ESV)

We further declare:

"We have sinned and done wrong and acted wickedly and rebelled, turning aside from your commandments and rules. We have not listened to your servants the prophets, who spoke in your name to our kings, our princes, and our fathers, and to all the people of the land. To you, O Lord, belongs righteousness, but to us open shame, as at this day, to the men of Judah, to the inhabitants of Jerusalem, and to all Israel, those who are near and those who are far away, in all the lands to which you have driven them, because of the treachery that they [we] have committed against you. To us, O Lord, belongs open shame, to our kings, to our princes, and to our fathers, because we have sinned against you. To the Lord our God belong mercy and forgiveness, for we have rebelled against him and have not obeyed the voice of the Lord our God by walking in his laws [Torah], which he set before us by his servants the prophets. All Israel has transgressed your law [Torah] and turned aside, refusing to obey Your voice. And the curse and oath that are written in the Law of Moses [Torah] the servant of God have been poured out upon us, because we have sinned against Him." DANIEL 9:5-11 (ESV)

Holy One of Israel, we are guilty!

"Both we and our fathers have sinned; we have committed iniquity; we have done wickedness." PSALM 106:6 (ESV)

We agree with Isaiah:

"For your hands are defiled with blood and your fingers with iniquity; your lips have spoken lies; your tongue mutters wickedness." ISAIAH 59:3 (ESV)

But, we plead, along with Isaiah:

> *"Be not so terribly angry, O Lord, and remember not iniquity forever. Behold, please look, we are all your people."* ISAIAH 64:9 (ESV)

You said to Ezekiel:

> *"Son of man, when the house of Israel lived in their own land, they defiled it by their ways and their deeds. Their ways before me were like the uncleanness of a woman in her menstrual impurity."* EZEKIEL 36:17 (ESV)

> *"I dealt with them according to their uncleanness and their transgressions, and hid my face from them."* EZEKIEL 39:24 (ESV)

As You promised Moses, Your faithful servant, so You have done:

> *"I will hide my face from them; I will see what their end will be, for they are a perverse generation, children in whom is no faithfulness."* DEUTERONOMY 32:20 (ESV)

We who have seen our vast crookedness now cry out with David's prayer:

> *"Have mercy on me, O God, according to Your steadfast love; according to your abundant mercy blot out my transgressions. Wash me thoroughly from my iniquity, and cleanse me from my sin! For I know my transgressions, and my sin is ever before me. Against you, you only, have I sinned and done what is evil in your sight, so that you may be justified in your words and blameless in your judgment. Behold, I was brought forth in iniquity, and in sin did my mother conceive me."* PSALM 51:1-5 (ESV)

Merciful YEHOVAH, Elohim of Israel, we agree that both we and our Church forefathers have been stubborn, stiff-necked, perverse, rebellious, deceitful, and utterly wicked. We have bowed down to idols, cast off Your Word, and despised Your covenant of shalom. We are guilty of every abomination. It is only because of Your covenant with Abraham, Isaac, and Jacob, and, for the sake of Your great name, that we have not been utterly destroyed!

O Holy One, thank You for forgiveness! Please restore us! Would you please gather us from among the nations where You have scattered us? Vindicate the holiness of Your great name, so that the nations will know that You are YEHOVAH, Elohim of Israel! (Ezekiel 36:22-23, 37:21)

You have promised mercy to a thousand generations (Deuteronomy 7:9, 1 Chronicles 16:15, Psalm 105:8) and You said:

> *"But the mercy of the LORD is from everlasting to everlasting upon them that fear him, his righteousness unto children's children."* PSALM 103:17 (ESV)

Elohim of Abraham, Isaac, and Jacob, may all Israel and the nations enter into Your covenant and be saved and restored!

Restore us also to our elder brother, Judah.

> *"Then shall the children of Judah and the children of Israel be gathered together and appoint themselves one head."* HOSEA 1:11 (ESV)

Make us ONE, all for Your glory!

Amein and amein!

Christian Contributors - Name, Ministry and Contact Information

1. Nathalie Blackham and her husband Martin are presenters of the Israel First TV Programme, which focuses on news, interviews and features from Israel, along with teaching from a Hebraic perspective. Since 2004 they have been producing their programmes from the Israel First TV Studios in Jerusalem, Israel.

Their Israel First TV Programme is broadcast every Friday on Angel TV via satellite on the following channels: Australia, Far East, Hebrew, Portuguese, Spanish and America. It is also broadcast on Watchmen Broadcasting, CTN Big Bend TV45 Network, GLC and Israel TV Network.

Website: http://www.israelfirst.org
Email: info@israelfirst.org

2. Linda Chandler is the ordained pastor at Austin Brethren Church. Linda has a B.S.Ed from the University of Texas, an M.S.Ed from The University of Houston, and an M.Div from Austin Presbyterian Theological Seminary. Today, she pastors her local congregation as a "House of Prayer" with an emphasis on healing love and deep biblical discipleship. She is the founder and Executive Officer of HOST Ministries (www.hostministries.org) which serves as a catalyst and tool in uniting people for God's purposes, especially Christians and Jews. In 2014 she published her first book, "Gates of Redemption".

Website: www.hostministries.org
Email: contact her through hostministries.org website

3. Thomas and Amy Cogdell lead a community of prayer called Christ the Reconciler. Though they grew up together in the same Protestant church, the Lord led Amy into the Roman Catholic Church in the year 2000. Since then they have felt called to a ministry of healing, reconciliation and spiritual formation among Christians of different traditions. They became aware of the importance of Jew/Gentile reconciliation during the Wittenberg 2017 initiative, which culminated at the 500th anniversary of the Protestant Reformation on October 31st, 2017.

They have five children, three grandchildren, and a desire to extend a warm welcome to anyone who would like to visit them in Texas.

Website: http://www.christthereconciler.org
Email: amycogdell@gmail.com

4. Jeff Daly is a former Wall Street lawyer, atheist, and New-Ager. In 1991, Jeff had an epiphany, repented, and followed Christ. Since 1999, with his wife Laurie, he has pastored - and now is Director - of Jesus Christ Fellowship, in Middletown, California. He practices law and is a director of Capitol Hill Prayer Partners.

In 2009, he wrote "The Spiritual Battle for the White House." In 2011, he founded National Day of Repentance, www.repentday.com, to encourage personal and national repentance by which the Lord can purify His people and heal their land. His new book "Call on God's Protection, Mr. President" urges President Trump to call for a national Day of Repentance.

Website: http://repentday.com
Email: PastorJeff@repentday.com

5. Christine Darg is co-founder with her husband Peter, of The Jerusalem Channel. They are broadcast journalists, and their call to Israel was confirmed in 1978 when they were selected by the Christian Broadcasting Network (CBN) to open a news bureau in Jerusalem. Today, Christine's ministry at www.JerusalemChannel.tv reaches out globally from Jerusalem to all nations via Revelation TV and The Jerusalem Channel teaching about Israel and End Time events. At least three times a year Christine brings groups to Israel for life-changing insider tours during Passover and the Feast of Tabernacles, and other prayer convocations and prophetic conferences.

Website: https://jerusalemchannel.tv
Email: cdarg1@me.com

6. Laura Densmore (editor/co-author) is founder of Daily Audio Torah, a website where one can listen to daily audios and journey through the entire bible in one year focusing on the biblical calendar, the feasts and the Torah reading cycle. Laura is also founder and director of Bridge Connector Ministries, whose primary goal is to build a bridge between Jews and Christians — beginning with Christian repentance for the sins of our Church forefathers.

Website: https://bridgeconnectorministries.com
Website: https://www.dailyaudiotorah.com
Email: bridgeconnectorministries@gmail.com

7. Cathy Helms is an intercessor and part-time blogger. Many years after God began to open her eyes more fully to His kingdom by inviting her to participate in His Sabbaths and feasts, she began to share with others by way of The Wilderness Report.

Website: http://www.cathyhelms.com
Email: cathy@cathyhelms.com

8. Sister Joela and Sister Damiana are with the Evangelical Sisterhood of Mary.

The destruction of Darmstadt in 1944 brought the first generation of their community into confrontation with the holiness of God. But the ruins left by World War II were to become the birthplace of new spiritual life. Their aim is to carry the message of reconciliation far beyond the boundaries of nations, cultures and denominations, and to prepare the Bride from Israel and the nations for the coming of the Messiah. In 2001, The Evangelical Sisterhood of Mary initiated and organized a repentance service in Jerusalem at Ramat Rachel. They have had a physical presence in the Land of Israel since 1957.

Website: www.kanaan.org
Email: S.Joela@kanaan.org and S.Damiana@kanaan.org

9. Donna Jollay is a hi-tech entrepreneur, philanthropist, and, most dear to her heart, is a deeply committed Christian Zionist. The Jewish people are HaShem's chosen vessel to bring Himself and His Word into this world. As such, Christians owe them a huge debt of gratitude, but instead have treated them terribly for 2,000 years. Donna has dedicated her life to doing what she can to rectify this, by bridging the Christian and Jewish communities. In 2015 she co-founded Yeshiva For The Nations with Rabbi Tuly Weisz of Israel365.

Yeshiva for the Nations is an online academy that offers authentic Torah classes designed specifically for non-Jews. All course offerings, both online and on site, are taught by Orthodox Jews from Israel, and are designed for those interested in dipping into the wellsprings of Jewish learning. It is a project of Israel365, which promotes the beauty and religious significance of Israel to friends and supporters around the world.

Website: www.yeshivaforthenations.com
Email: info@yeshivaforthenations.com

10. Albert J. McCarn is the Executive Director of Bney Yosef North America, which is an organization dedicated to the awakening of Hebrew identity among the people of the Lord God (YHVH), and the promised reunion of the House of Yosef/Ephraim (the non-Jewish part of Israel) with our Jewish brethren who have remained the core of God's covenant nation.

We are dedicated completely to Yeshua of Nazareth, whom we understand to be the Messiah. It is by Him we are redeemed and included in covenant relationship with the Almighty. It is by his atoning work that we have a part in the Commonwealth of Israel as the returning "Lost Sheep of the House of Israel".

Website: https://bneyyosefna.com
Email: info@bneyyosefna.com

11. Ray Montgomery (co-author) is a researcher, writer, and co-author of The LIST. In 2008 he began compiling a Christian Timeline to get a sense of the "Big Picture" of Church history. In 2010, he began researching Jewish history as well. This ultimately led to a personal journey of repentance, which in turn led to a heart reconciliation with his Jewish brethren. In March 2018 he felt compelled to contact Bob O'Dell, whose journey had mirrored his own, in the hopes that Bob would "do something" to bring this knowledge to a wider Christian audience. Bob invited his collaboration, and together they produced The LIST, which prompted Laura Densmore to propose these 40 daily devotions based on their findings.

Email: ray@root-source.com

12. Amy Mucklestone is a volunteer publications editor and proofreader with HaYovel, and her husband Thomas is their longest-standing board member since 2010. HaYovel is a Christian organization based in the USA that brings volunteers from all around the world to participate in the prophetic Restoration of Israel by serving Israeli farmers in Judea and Samaria. Their work includes educating the nations about God's ongoing covenants with the land and people of Israel.

Website: https://www.hayovel.com
Email: info@hayovel.com

13. Bob O'Dell (co-author) is co-founder of Root-Source.com. Today, more and more Christians and Jews are hearing the divine call to wake up and engage with one another.

Root Source is answering that call: knowledgeable, Orthodox Israeli Jews are teaching Christians around the world online about Jewish concepts, ideas and thought, to more deeply understand the roots of their faith, in an informal and loving manner.

Root Source enables and encourages dialogue and relationships between Christians and Jews, and empowers Christians to learn as Jews have been learning for centuries. Their Israeli Jewish teachers know you are a Christian, and respect your identity and your faith.

Website: https://root-source.com
Website: https://9-av.com
Email: bob@root-source.com

14. Sharon Sanders and her husband Ray are the co-founders of the ministry Christian Friends of Israel, one of the major pioneering Christian Zionist ministries in the Land of Israel. It is an international evangelical Christian ministry legally registered in Israel, with headquarters in Jerusalem, where they operate multiple outreaches and administer the ministry. They also have representative offices throughout the world.

CFI represents Christians worldwide who love Israel, and who desire to express friendship and a united stand with Israel based on the Bible. CFI's main objectives are to take the love of Jesus back to the people who brought it to us, which they do through outreach projects in Israel.

Website: http://christianfriendsofisrael.org
Email: cfi@cfijerusalem.org

15. Steve Wearp works with Blessed Buy Israel, whose ministry focus is to provide a way for people around the world to stand with the Jewish people against the existential threat posed by those who promote the destruction of Israel through the BDS movement (Boycott, Divest and Sanction).

Blessed Buy Israel Ministries is dedicated to educating and empowering people to stand with the Jewish communities in Israel, as they endeavor to live out the covenants and promises given to them by God. Our goal is to encourage people around the world to embrace the common roots of our faith in the God of Abraham, and provide practical ways to assist and support the Jewish people and communities as they endeavor to rebuild, restore and protect their families, heritage and nation.

Website: https://blessedbuyisrael.com
Email: Steve@blessedbuyisrael.com

56179938R00142

Made in the USA
Middletown, DE
20 July 2019